HOW
TO SERVE
ON A JURY

By

PHILIP FRANCIS

OCEANA PUBLICATIONS

43 West 16th Street   New York 11, N. Y.

This is the thirty-first number of the LEGAL ALMANAC SERIES which will bring the law on various subjects to you in non-technical language. These books do not take the place of your attorney's advice, but they can introduce you to your legal rights and responsibilities.

OCEANA PUBLICATIONS

Library of Congress Catalog Card Number: 53-5766

TABLE OF CONTENTS

Chapter One

PAGE

WHAT IS A JURY? 5
Number of jurors 5
Origin and history of the jury.................................. 6
Prevalence of the jury system.................................. 10
Constitutional rights of the jury.............................. 10

Chapter Two

THE FUNCTIONS OF THE JURY.............................. 12
General: The duties of jurors.................................. 12
Criminal cases 17
The jury as assessors of damages 18
Functions of the Grand Jury 19
Coroner's jury 19

Chapter Three

WHO IS THE JURY? 20
Sex of the prospective juror.................................. 20
Chart No. 1—Service of women as jurors........... 21
Age of the prospective juror................................. 22
Chart No. 2—Maximum and minimum ages of
jurors 23
Civil status 24
Color 24
Citizenship 25
Literacy 25
Occupations 25
Chart No. 3—Occupations exempt, disqualified
and required to serve as jurors.......................... 69

Chapter Four

SELECTION OF THE JURY 26
Preliminary selection 26
Special juries 26
Selection for trial 27
Challenges 29
Alternate jurors 31
Disqualification after selection 33

TABLE OF CONTENTS (Continued)   PAGE

Excuses 33
The foreman 34

Chapter Five

THE DUTIES AND PRIVILEGES OF A JUROR 36
Attendace 36
Seating 36
Hearing the evidence 37
Objections 38
Jurors' discussion of the case 39
Independent investigations 39
Asking questions 42
Taking notes 42
Retiring to the jury room 43
Your deliberations as jurors 43
Evaluating witnesses 45
Consideration of damages and sentence 47
Sentences and recommendations of mercy 48
General 49
Meals 50
Lodging 50
Mileage and compensation 50
Length of deliberations 51

Chapter Six

THE VERDICT 52
Unanimity of the verdict 52
Returning the verdict 55
Sealed verdicts 56
Finality of the verdict 57
Impeaching the verdict 57

Chapter Seven

MILITARY JURIES (TRIAL BY COURTS-MARTIAL) 59
Comparison of military and civil courts 59
Limitations on powers of military courts 60
Selection of members of courts-martial 61
Challenges 62
Voting and deliberations 63
JURORS' GLOSSARY 76

Chapter One

WHAT IS A JURY

In your state the sheriff or deputy sheriff may bring you a little white, green or pink slip of paper summoning you to appear for duty as a member of the jury—in mine it may be received in the morning mail, but in both your state and mine, we are called to perform one of the most important and interesting of our duties as citizens. We are at the same time being summoned to perform an obligation, and invited to exercise one of the privileges which is peculiar to the democratic form of government—participation in trial by jury.

A JURY is a body of men or women—or both—who are sworn to declare the facts of a case as they are proven from the evidence placed before them. A juror is, strictly speaking, a person who has been selected to serve on a jury, and who has been sworn to serve in a particular case, although the term also is applied loosely to a person who has received a summons to report for jury duty.

NUMBER OF JURORS

A jury, depending upon the purpose for which it is called, and the court in which it is to serve, will have anywhere from six to twenty-four members. The larger number serves only when a Grand Jury is called. The Grand Jury does not sit for the conduct of a trial or hear the evidence for both sides of a case. It is merely an accusing body or group of citizens to whom alleged offenses are referred for action. While the number of Grand Jurors varies in different states, the usual practice is to swear twenty-three members, so there will not be an even division of opinion. In most states, the concurrence of twelve members of the jury, and not merely a majority of those present, is necessary before the grand jury may perform an effective or valid act. After twenty-three grand jurors have been selected to serve, and sworn for a specified term, usually for a month, the prosecuting attorney presents to the jury witnesses to the alleged crimes. After the evidence has been presented, the prosecuting officer retires, and the grand jury votes on whether a written accusation of an offense is to be made. Unlike a trial or petit jury, all of whose members must be present before any action may be taken at any stage of the proceedings, a grand jury may function as long as a majority of its members are present. Regardless of the number present, or absent, however, there must be twelve jurors in agreement before the written accusation of an offense may be returned. If there are twelve grand jurors in agreement, the grand jury is said to have "returned a true bill", or an indictment, while if twelve jurors do not concur, the grand jury is said to have "returned no bill".

While the grand jury consists, as a general rule, of twenty-three members, some of whom may be absent during its proceedings, and only twelve of whom need concur for a valid result, the jury which sits and serves as the judge of the facts at a trial, and which is known as a trial or petit jury, usually consists of twelve members, all of whom must be present during all stages of the trial or other proceeding. While the old rule of unanimous verdicts has been somewhat relaxed in recent years in some states, the verdicts will be dealt with in more detail in Chapter Six. In some jurisdictions, and particularly in courts of inferior jurisdiction, where less serious criminal offenses are tried, and where the amount sued for does not exceed three thousand dollars, a jury may consist of only six members.

ORIGIN AND HISTORY OF THE JURY SYSTEM

The Chief of the small, primitive tribe was the ruler, the legislature, and both the trial court and the court of last resort. He was both the judge and the jury, and decided questions of fact along with questions of law. As long as the tribe was small, he was in a position to have all the facts, and he was the law. As the tribe increased, and as the power of the chief diminished, his decision was modified and influenced by the elders or outstanding warriors of the

6

tribe, and in many cases by the judgment of the tribe itself. In some tribes, there evolved a rough system of tribal justice in which the entire tribe participated, serving as the judges both of the law and of the facts, while in other tribes the chief or the elders sat as the judges of the law while the entire tribe, or the men of the tribe, sat as judges of the facts. The rules of the tribe were elastic, and were by no means uniform. The jury, as it functioned, might vary both as to number and as to the composition of its members.

In ancient Greece, we found a large, and sometimes unwieldly, but nevertheless definite and workable jury system, in many respects surprisingly similar to the jury as we know it today. In Athens, a jury list of six thousand or more names was made up each year. This was the list which corresponded to our modern jury lists, where, for instance, in Bronx County, in New York State, there is a list of twenty-six thousand jurors. In some less populous counties where the Court sits only three months out of every twelve, the list may be as small as three hundred. Some counties publish small booklets listing the attorneys who try cases in the county, and the jurors called for each term or session of the court. In Athens, for ordinary cases, two hundred and one names were drawn by lot as a panel for the trial, while in special cases the panel might be as large as five hundred or even a thousand. In the case in which Socrates was condemned to death for impiety and corruption of youth, five hundred and one jurors voted, and he was found guilty by a majority of sixty. While there were magistrates who supervised the preliminaries, at the trial itself the Athenian magistrate was no more than the chairman of a public assembly. There was no presiding judge to declare the law, and no appeal in the modern sense. The citizens were the whole court—the judges of the law as well as of the facts, and there was no jury deliberation. Under the jury system as we know it, after the conclusion of the evidence, the closing speeches by the lawyers, and the Court's instructions or charge to the jury, the jury retires to deliberate, and then, after a longer or shorter period of discussion and balloting, returns to the

Court with its verdict. In Athens, as soon as the speeches were completed, the jurors filed out, and on the way out cast their ballots. In criminal cases, upon entering the trial, the jurors were given two ballots—one for guilty and one for acquittal. One ballot was cast into the "voting urn", and the other into the 'discard urn." In civil cases, where one party (the plaintiff) asked for money or other damages from another (the defendant), the jurors were provided with a plaintiff's ballot and a defendant's ballot. As a rule, a bronze or brass urn received the effective ballots, while the discarded or ineffective ballots, which were not to count, were cast into the wooden discard urn. After the jurors had voted, the attendants counted the ballots, and announced the verdict. If the ballots should happen to be equal in number, the verdict was for the defendant, whether the case was civil or criminal. If the verdict was for the plaintiff in a civil case, or was a verdict of guilty in a criminal case, a second ballot was conducted, to determine the amount of damages in a civil case, or the sentence in a criminal case.

In the Roman legal system, evolved somewhat from the Greek, in the early days the entire popular assembly might sit in judgment, and there was in effect a system of sixty thousand jurors voting on a single case. The democratic system evolved smaller juries, selected by lot as in Greece, but under the emperors lay juries disappeared, and most trials, both civil and criminal, took place under a single judge.

On the European Continent we found lay juries in Germany, sitting with the baron, seneschal, or sheriff in order to voice the sentiment of popular justice. In Germany, as in Athens, the more primitive tribal custom of doing justice by the votes of all freemen in the assembly had become impracticable and had suffered a similar simmering down to a selected few. These lay judges, called "schoffen" in Germany, "échevins" in France, "scabini" in Italy, and eventually "doomsmen" or "jurors" in English, originally declared what custom required, and pronounced the judgment both of law and of fact. Under the emperor Charlemagne the jurors, by whatever name they were called, were

8

a select permanent list. In Germany, it was the jurors, and not the presiding baron, who pronounced the judgment, both on the law and on the facts.

Trial by Jury came slowly to the British Isles, from whence in time it was transported to America during colonial times. The Normans brought with them from France modified forms of their own trial by jury, but the jury, as it first appeared in England, was far removed from the jury as we know it today. A present day juror must approach the trial with an open mind—if he knows anything of substance about the case for which he is called he will be disqualified. The early juror in England was much more of a witness than a juror, and the name of the jury originally was 'juré", the French word for "sworn". The jurors, far from coming with open minds, were called and sworn as witnesses, and their verdict was their sworn testimony. The judgment of a jury was slow to be accepted, and as late as the thirteenth century trial by battle still ranked above trial by jury as a medium of settling disputes. When the Church forbade trial by ordeal in 1219, trial by jury took an important step forward, judges began to press jurors for an exact answer, and the defense began to present its own witnesses in addition to the testimony of the jurors. The defense witnesses, at times were part of the jury, and at other times merely heard by the jury, who then weighed and considered the defense evidence. When difficulties arose in reconciling different versions, the jury called its own witnesses, and gradually evolved, at about the fifteenth century, into a body which heard witnesses but did not itself bear witness or testify. While the growth of the jury system in England took the direction of the jury passing on the facts, and calling on the judge for instruction as to the law of the case, on the continent the frequent asking of advice by the jurors resulted in the increase of the functions of the judge, and the gradual elimination of the jury. On the continent the judicial system took the direction of a court composed of several judges, while in England the single judge and jury system grew in popularity and prevalence.

The jury system, as brought by the Colonists to America, was at times a potent instrument in the struggle for independence, and juries effectively thwarted the enforcement of unpopular British laws by refusing to return verdicts of guilty despite clear evidence of violation of law.

PREVALENCE OF THE JURY SYSTEM

While the jury system is accepted in the United States as a matter of course, as well as a matter of right, and exists in the British Isles, it is by no means a universally accepted means of determining disputes. In the non-English speaking countries where trial by jury is permitted, it is usually limited to the trial of criminal offenses. In Belgium, criminal and political charges, and offenses of the press are tried before a jury, while trial by jury has existed in Greece since 1834. In Norway, there has been trial by jury in criminal cases since 1887, but only a majority is required for a conviction. In Sweden, it is limted to offenses of the press, while in France and Italy serious criminal cases are tried by jury. In Germany, under local government, and before the occupation by the conquering powers, trial by jury was provided in all criminal cases except treason, political crimes and offenses of the press. The South American republics have all adopted trial by jury in criminal cases.

CONSTITUTIONAL RIGHT TO TRIAL BY JURY

The Sixth and Seventh Amendments of the United States Constitution guarantee the right to trial by jury in both criminal and civil cases, while the Fifth Amendment provided that except in cases arising in the land or naval forces, and in the militia, no person shall be held to answer for a capital or otherwise infamous crime except upon indictment or presentment by a Grand Jury. ,

In civil cases, the right to trial by jury is preserved in suits at Common Law where the amount in controversy exceeds twenty dollars. In criminal cases the Sixth Amendment expressly provides:

'In all criminal prosecutions, the accused shall enjoy the right to a speedy and public trial, by an impartial jury of the State and district where the crime shall have been committed, which district shall have been previously ascertained by law, and to be informed of the nature and cause of the accusation; to be confronted with the witnesses against him, to have compulsory process for obtaining witnesses in his favor, and to have the Assistance of Counsel for his defence."

Most state constitutions have similar provisions preserving this right in which Americans take such pride. Persons charged with offenses committed under the jurisdiction of the Armed Forces are tried by a Court Martial, which, except for comparatively minor offenses, are a form of trial by jury. Minor military offenses are tried by a Summary Court Martial, where one officer of the Armed Forces sits as judge both of the law and of the facts. More serious offenses are tried by Special Courts Martial, where the president of the Court, who is to a certain extent a judge, is also a member who deliberates with the other members of the Court, and passes with them on questions of fact in the same manner as a juror in civilian courts. Major offenses are tried by a General Court Martial, which consists of a Law Officer, who is not a member of the Court, and a minimum of five members.

It is worthy of note that the Seventh Amendment limits this absolute right to a trial by jury to "suits at common law where the value in controversy shall exceed twenty dollars." Where the case is brought in equity, as, for example, for a decree or order ordering a defendant to perform a contract, or by a wife for a decree of separation from her husband, there is no constitutional right, and in most states, no statutory right to a trial by jury. A judge may, however, if he feels that the interests of justice will be better served, direct a trial by a jury of some or all of the disputed questions of fact in an equity case. A typical example of such procedure is where in an action for a divorce, there has been a charge of adultery. Under such circumstances we say that there has been a "framing of the issues", or of the question whether one of the spouses did or did not commit adultery, and where the issue has been framed, it will be decided by a jury.

Chapter Two

THE FUNCTIONS OF THE JURY

GENERAL

THE DUTIES OF JURORS

Trial by jury is lauded as the typical American democratic way of administering justice. In criminal cases, the jury decides whether a person accused of a crime or other offense is to be deprived of his life, or of his liberty for a certain period of time. In most cases the jury does not determine the punishment, but merely returns a verdict of guilty or not guilty. In the case of a verdict of guilty, the judge then imposes sentence, usually but not always following the recommendations of the jury. Disputes or controversies between one person and another, such as a suit for damages caused by an automobile accident, are also decided by a jury. In such a case the jury not only decides who is to be the winner, but also, by its verdict, fixes the amount of the "winnings".

In every contested lawsuit, there is a plaintiff, who has brought the suit and who has asked for relief, and a defendant, who is the person or firm named as the one or ones against whom relief is asked. If John Walker is struck and injured by Dave Driver's automobile, and Driver will not pay Walker's hospital bills or his lost wages, Walker will sue Driver, and the name of the case will be

John Walker
        Plaintiff
    against
David Driver
        Defendant

Walker will ask the jury to return a verdict, and to say not only that they find, as he claims, that the injury was caused solely by Driver's fault, without any fault on Walker's part, but also to determine the amount of damages which Walker has suffered and which Driver must pay. There may be more than one plaintiff, and more than one defendant. If Ralph Rider and Mary Rider, his wife and Fred Friend, were passengers in a taxicab owned and driven by Curt Carrier, and the taxi collided with Dave Driver's car because of the fault of both drivers, the name or title of the case would be

Ralph Rider, Mary Rider and Fred Friend

Plaintiffs

against

Curt Carrier and David Driver

Defendants.

The "plaintiffs" are the people who bring the lawsuit, while the "defendants" are the ones who resist or defend against the claim or claims made by the plaintiffs. The plaintiff begins the lawsuit by serving on the defendant a summons and complaint. The complaint is a sworn statement of the plaintiff's claim against the defendant or defendants, stating the facts on which the plaintiff or plaintiffs rely for their recovery, the reasons why they claim that the defendant or defendants should be required to pay damages, and the amount of damages. The defendant then has a certain number of days, varying from state to state, within which to serve his answer, or sworn statement telling why he believes that he should not be required to pay anything. The defendant is not limited in his answer to a defense against the claims made by the plaintiff, but he may at the same time "counterclaim", and ask that the Court, in denying the plaintiff any right to recover against him, award him a sum of money to be paid by the plaintiff. If there is a counterclaim served by the defendant, the plaintiff will then serve a "reply" or statement telling why he believes that the defendant should not be awarded any damages on his counterclaim. The pleadings consist of the complaint (also called in some states, the "bill of complaint", "declaration", "writ"), the answer, and the reply. The pleadings determine just what disputed questions of fact there are to be tried and determined by the jury, and what questions of law are to be determined by the Court. Occasionally the pleadings, or some of the pleadings will be handed to the jury for their inspection or consideration.

Not all of the facts pleaded or stated in the complaint, answer and reply will be tried by the jury. Suppose, for instance, that the plaintiff served a complaint asking for money damages because the defendant broke an agreement to deliver lumber. In the complaint the plaintiff sets forth the agreement and the acts or omissions of the defendant which the plaintiff claims breached or abrogated the agreement. If the defendant denies everything, the jury must first decide whether there was an agreement, and if there was an agreement, whether the defendant broke the agreement, then, if he broke the agreement, what damages the plaintiff suffered. Suppose, however, that the defendant admits the agreement, but claims that he did not break it. The jury will not, under such circumstances, be required to consider whether there was an agreement, but only whether there was a breach of the agreement. The same situation may arise in an automobile accident case, where the driver of the car involved admits that he owned and operated the car, but denies that it was his fault. The jury will then be obliged to consider only the question of fault, or liability and damages, whereas if the defendant denied ownership and control of the car, and claimed that some other car and driver were involved, and not he, the jury would have to consider first whether it was the defendant who was involved in the accident, and after considering that question, would then consider the questions of fault and liability and, if they found in favor of the plaintiff, the question of damages.

After the pleadings have been served, and the case has been placed on the Court calendar for trial, the Court will fix a date for trial. On the date fixed by the Court, a panel of jurors will be summoned and the parties (the plaintiff and the defendant) will appear with their lawyers, or counsel, as the lawyers are called by the Court. In large cities, such as New York, Philadelphia and Chicago, where a great many cases are tried simultaneously in different "Parts" or rooms of the Court, with a separate judge and jury presiding in each part, several hundred jurors may be summoned at one time, and the jurors selected in a central "Jury Part" and then conducted to the particular courtroom where they will try their case, but in most states and jurisdictions, the number of jurors to be called will be only sufficient to provide for twelve jurors remaining after both sides have used up their "challenges" and have excused those prospective jurors whom they do not hesitate to have on the jury. (See Chapter IV for an explanation of "Challenges".) The jury to try a particular case will be selected by the opposing lawyers, under the supervision of the judge (or, in Federal Courts, by the Judge with suggestions made by the lawyers, and challenges exercised by the lawyers), and after selection to the satisfaction of both sides, the jury will be sworn and the case begun.

At the beginning of the trial, the lawyer for the plaintiff will make an opening statement to the Court and Jury. In this opening statement, referred to as his "Opening", the plaintiff's lawyer gives an outline of his case, telling the jury just what he expects to prove, and the evidence and testimony by which he expects to prove it. The detail with which he explains his case will, of course, vary according to the nature and circumstances of the case and the plan of the lawyer. Whether the opening is long or short, however, the jurors should listen attentively, since it will let them know what to expect. They should remember, however, that the opening is not evidence, but a statement of what evidence will be produced to prove the facts stated in the opening. After the plaintiff's lawyer has finished his opening, the lawyer for the defendant will make an opening statement, in which he will tell the jury the contention of his client, and what evidence he intends to produce to resist the plaintiff's claim.,

After the opening statements of the lawyers, the first witness will be called. The plaintiff's witnesses will be called first, and as each witness is called he is asked questions first by the lawyer calling him to the witness stand. These

15

questions by the lawyer who calls a witness are said to constitute his "direct examination", and when the lawyer has finished asking his questions of the witness, he turns to the lawyer for the other side and says: "Your witness", "You may cross examine", or "You may inquire". The lawyer for the other side then asks questions which try to bring out further facts, to contradict, or to explain facts concerning which the witness has made answers on his direct examination. He may also ask the witness questions which "affect his credibility". The lawyer hopes and expects that the answers to these questions will tend to show that the answers of the witness on his direct examination should either be rejected, because the witness is unworthy of belief, or accepted with skepticism, because the witness has shown by his answers that there is doubt concerning either his truthfulness or his bias in favor of one of the parties, or his hostility toward another. The plaintiff presents his case, and calls his witness first. After he calls each witness to the witness chair, the witness is sworn, in the presence of the Court, jury and all parties, and, after giving his name and address to the Court reporter, the plaintiff's lawyer conducts the "direct examination," the defendant's lawyer conducts his "cross examination," the plaintiff's lawyer, if he so desires, conducts a "redirect examination," and, in some instances, the defendant's lawyer conducts a "recross examination." This procedure is followed in the case of each witness, and after the plaintiff has called all his witnesses, his lawyer tells the Court that "the plaintiff rests." The defendant's lawyer then asks the Court to dismiss the case, and if the judge decides that he wants to have arguments on the rules of law involved in the case, the jury will be excused for a few minutes while the lawyers argue points of law before the judge. If, as happens in the vast majority of cases, the motion is denied, the defendants lawyer then calls his witnesses, and takes them through their direct examination. Each witness is cross examined, and after the defendant has called all his witnesses, he tells the court that "the defendant rests." After the defense rests, or finishes its case, the plaintiff's lawyer may call witnesses in rebuttal or reply to the defendants witnesses, and thereafter both sides will rest.

After both sides have rested, and the evidence is closed, the lawyer for each side makes a summing up speech to the jury in support of his client. In most states the defendant makes the first summing up speech or "summation", and the plaintiff the last. In some states this is varied, with the plaintiff making the first and the defendant the last speech, while in a few states the summations are divided into an "opening argument" by the plaintiff, an argument by the defendant, and a "closing Argument" by the plaintiff.

After both sides have completed their arguments, the judge then instructs or "charges" the jury, giving them their instructions on law. The jurors are bound to accept the law as explained to them by the judge, but are at liberty to reach their own verdict on the facts. If they do not agree with the judge's outline or recollection of the facts, they may disregard it in whole or in part, since the jurors' own recollection is controlling.

CRIMINAL CASES

Prosecutions in criminal cases are brought in the name of the people of a state, or the people of the United States as plaintiff against a person, persons or sometimes a corporation as defendants. The reason for the prosecution of a case is that the persons or corporations charged are claimed to have committed a crime or serious offense against the public generally. While the offense charged is claimed to have been committed against the public generally, it may also have been a wrong or injury to a specific person or persons. An offense such as assault or armed robbery, while an offense against the public welfare generally, is also an offense against a private individual, and the individual wronged is not precluded from maintaining a civil case against the defendant by the fact that the State or Federal Government has brought criminal charges.

In a criminal case, it is the duty and the obligation of the jury to decide whether the defendant is guilty or not guilty of the charge or charges on which he is being tried. Evidence in support of the charge made against the defendant is introduced by the prosecutor, usually the District Attorney, or Assistant District Attorney, in the case of State prosecutions, and the United States Attorney or Assisant United States Attorney in the case of Federal prosecutions.

The procedure is substantially similar to that followed in civil cases. After the jury is selected, the prosecutor makes an opening statement, and the defendant's lawyer may either make his opening immediately, or wait until the prosecution has rested its case. After direct examination by each witness is completed by the prosecutor, the defendant's lawyer is given an opportunity to cross examine, and, as in civil cases, the cross examination may be followed by redirect examination by the prosecuting attorney. After the prosecution has rested, the defendant presents his witnesses, who are examined by his lawyer and cross examined by the prosecutor, with the privilege of redirect examination by the defendant's lawyer. After the defendant has rested, the prosecution may call witnesses and offer evidence in rebuttal, and when both sides have rested and have no further evidence, the lawyers deliver their closing arguments to the jury. After the arguments the judge instructs or charges the jury as in a civil case, and the jury retires to its deliberations to determine the guilt or innocence of the defendant.

In a few states the jury not only determines guilt or innocence, but also fixes the sentence. This practice, however, is the exception rather than the rule, and in most states, and in all Federal prosecutions, the judge imposes the sentence after the jury has returned a verdict of guilty.

THE JURY AS ASSESSORS OF DAMAGES

In some cases there is no issue of fact except the amount of damages. Suppose, for example, that the jurors are serving in a case where the plaintiff is asking for damages for breach of contract. If the undisputed facts shows that the plaintiff and the defendant made a binding contract, and that the defendant broke the contract, the only thing for the jury to determine will be the amount of damages to be awarded to the plaintiff. The jury's task may be the same where the defendant in an accident case has defaulted, or failed to serve an answer. The jury will then merely hear the plaintiff's witnesses, and will assess the damages which the plaintiff is to recover.

THE GRAND JURY

The Grand Jury, which usually consists of twenty-three members, is the accusing body of the government, state or Federal. Each County has its own grand jury, called for a term of a month, but often "held over" or continued for an additional month or more. The function of the Grand Jury is to determine whether a crime has been committed, and, if so, whether there is a reasonable probability that the defendant has committed the crime. The Grand Jury, as a general rule, hears only the witnesses called by the District Attorney or other prosecutor, and then determines, from the evidence before it, whether there is sufficient to make a formal accusation of a crime or other offense. If the jurors make an accusation of a felony, or serious crime, the accusation is called an "indictment", while if the accusation is a misdemeanor, the accusation may be called an "information". In cases where the grand jurors feel that while there is insufficient evidence to warrant an indictment or information, but where there has been some reprehensible conduct, or neglect or malfeasance of duty, the grand jurors may make a report or "presentment" calling for action by some governmental administrative body or agency.

CORONERS JURY

When a death has occurred under unusual or suspicious circumstances, the coroner of a county will convene a jury to hear evidence and to report on the cause of death. The jurors in such a case consider all the evidence which is presented to them, and return their verdict or report. The report is advisory only, and is not, by itself, evidence which may be used in a civil or criminal case. The evidence presented to the coroner's jury is, however, admissible in any civil or criminal case.

19

Chapter Three

WHO IS THE JURY

Service as a member of the jury is both a privilege and an obligation. It is a privilege to serve in the administration of justice, whether the particular case in which the juror is called concerns the liberty, or life of a defendant in a criminal prosecution, or the obligation of one citizen to pay money damages to another. It is a privilege which exists in part in only eleven countries in the world today, and in no country is the citizen given the privilege of having so large a say in the administration of justice as in the United States of America. Jury service is also an obligation in that a call to serve may not, in many instances, be denied. In determining who is to be on the jury, we may consider who may serve, who must serve, and who may not serve.

SEX OF THE PROSPECTIVE JUROR

In 1898 the State of Utah established a precedent by allowing women to serve on juries under certain conditions. Prior to that date, the right to serve on juries had been considered an exclusively male prerogative. Since the Utah innovation, however, theirty-seven other states, the District of Columbia and the Territory of Alaska, and Puerto Rico have enacted statutes permitting women to serve as jurors. In some jurisdictions, women are required to serve, and will not be permitted to be excused automatically solely because of their sex, while in others, they may serve if they so desire, or may stand upon a privilege extended to them, but not to male citizens generally, of being excused from jury service solely on the grounds of their sex.

In connection with women being excused from jury service we have a somewhat contradictory situation where service on juries in Federal Courts is concerned. In the nine states where women are ineligible to serve on juries, they are not called for service on Federal juries, and are not permitted to serve, even if they are willing to do so.

However, in Federal Courts sitting in states in which women are permitted, but not required to serve on State Court juries, women who may be called for service may not be excused merely because of their sex. They must have an excuse which the Federal Judge accepts as sufficient. As a practical matter, the judges are more lenient in excusing women than men, and will accept an excuse more readily where the juror asks relief from service because of illness or family emergencies.

In considering the eligibility of women as jurors, where not barred by state laws, Federal Commissioners of Jurors now exercise caution to avoid any basis for a charge that women may have been excluded from jury panels, or from the lists of Grand Jurors. Less than ten years ago an indictment for using the mails to defraud, brought against a woman in a state where women were permitted but not required to serve on state court juries, was dismissed because women had been systematically and arbitrarily excluded from service on the Grand Jury which returned the indictment, while in a later case an anti-trust indictment was dismissed on the same grounds in another Federal District. The states in which women MAY serve as jurors, as well as those in which they MUST serve, are set forth below in Chart I.

CHART I

State	May Women Serve?	Must Women Serve?
ALASKA	Yes	No
ARIZONA	Yes	No
ARKANSAS	Yes	No
CALIFORNIA	Yes	Yes
COLORADO	Yes	Yes
DISTRICT OF COLUMBIA	Yes	No
CONNECTICUT	Yes	No
DELAWARE	Yes	Yes
FLORIDA	Yes	No
IDAHO	Yes	No
ILLINOIS	Yes	Yes
IOWA	Yes	Yes
KANSAS	Yes	No
KENTUCKY	Yes	No
LOUISIANA	Yes	No

21

CHART I (Continued)

State	May Women Serve?	Must Women Serve?
MAINE	Yes	Yes
MARYLAND	Yes	Yes
MASSACHUSETTS	Yes	No
MICHIGAN	Yes	Yes
MINNESOTA	Yes	No
MISSOURI	Yes	No
MONTANA	Yes	Yes
NEBRASKA	Yes	Yes
NEVADA	Yes	No
NEW HAMPSHIRE	Yes	No
NEW JERSEY	Yes	Yes
NEW YORK	Yes	No
NORTH CAROLINA	Yes	Yes
NORTH DAKOTA	Yes	No
OHIO	Yes	Yes
OREGON	Yes	Yes
PENNSYLVANIA	Yes	Yes
RHODE ISLAND	Yes	No
UTAH	Yes	No
VERMONT	Yes	Yes
VIRGIN ISLANDS	Yes	No
WASHINGTON	Yes	Yes
WISCONSIN	Yes	No
WYOMING	Yes	Yes

In states where women MAY serve, a woman is permitted to refuse or decline to serve as a member of a jury panel solely on the basis of her sex. States where women MUST serve they are called for service in the same manner as male members of the panel. Women are wholly barred from jury service in local and Federal Courts sitting in Alabama, the Panama Canal Zone, Georgia, Hawaii, Mississippi, New Mexico, Oklahoma, South Carolina, Tennessee, Texas, Virginia and West Virginia.

AGE OF THE PROSPECTIVE JUROR

The age requirements vary in different states, although the most generally accepted practice is to accept for jury service from persons otherwise qualified those between the ages of twenty-one and seventy. Both the maximum and the minimum requirements vary, and we find some states which will not accept for jury service persons under the age of twenty-five years, and others which strike jurors from the lists on their attainment of the ages of sixty-five or even sixty years. The reasons advanced for the exclusion of youthful jurors is that they lack the necessary experience and understanding, while elderly jurors are sometimes excluded because they are generally believed to have lost some of their visual or auditory keenness. The statutes vary from state to state, and the details are set forth in Chart II, below:

CHART II

MAXIMUM AND MINIMUM AGE LIMITS FOR JURORS

State	Minimum Age	Maximum Age
ALABAMA	21	none—over 60 exempt
ALASKA	21	none
ARIZONA	21	none—over 60 exempt
ARKANSAS	21	none—over 65 exempt
CALIFORNIA	21	none
COLORADO	21	none
DISTRICT OF COLUMBIA	21	none
CONNECTICUT	25	none
DELAWARE	21	none
FLORIDA	21	none—over 60 exempt
GEORGIA	21	none—over 60 exempt
HAWAII	21	none—over 60 exempt
IDAHO	21	none
ILLINOIS	21	65
INDIANA	21	none—over 60 exempt
IOWA	21	none—over 65 exempt
KANSAS	21	none—over 65 exempt
KENTUCKY	21	none—over 60 exempt
LOUISIANA	21	none—over 60 exempt
MAINE	21	none
MARYLAND	25	None—over 70 exempt
MASSACHUSETTS	21	none—over 70 exempt
MICHIGAN	21	none—over 65 exempt
MINNESOTA	21	none—over 60 exempt
MISSISSIPPI	21	none
MISSOURI	21	none
MONTANA	21	70
NEBRASKA	25	70
NEVADA	21	none
NEW HAMPSHIRE	21	none—over 70 exempt
NEW JERSEY	21	65
NEW MEXICO	21	none—over 60 exempt
NEW YORK	21	70

CHART II (Continued)

State	Minimum Age	Maximum Age
NORTH CAROLINA	21	none
NORTH DAKOTA	21	none—over 60 exempt
OHIO	21	none
OKLAHOMA	21	60
OREGON	21	none
PENNSYLVANIA	21	none
PUERTO RICO	21	65
RHODE ISLAND	25	none—over 70 exempt
SOUTH CAROLINA	21	none—over 65 exempt
SOUTH DAKOTA	21	70
TENNESSEE	21	none—over 65 exempt
TEXAS	21	none—over 60 exempt
UTAH	21	none
VERMONT	21	none
VIRGINIA	21	none
VIRGIN ISLANDS	25	none
WASHINGTON	21	none—over 60 exempt
WEST VIRGINIA	21	65
WISCONSIN	21	none
WYOMING	21	65

CIVIL STATUS

In most states any person who has been convicted of a felony, or serious crime, will not be permitted to serve on a jury. In some states, the bar is raised only against those who have actually received a sentence of imprisonment for a year or more, or who have been guilty of certain types of offenses. The law of your own state will be explained to you when you are called to qualify as a juror. The most important point for any prospective juror to bear in mind is that he must not conceal any information which is sought by the authorities who ask him to qualify as a juror. This caution applies both when the information is sought in a written questionnaire, and when the prospective juror is answering questions asked by a clerk in the office of the Court or County Clerk. The convictions which will be sufficient to disqualify in your own state are shown in Chart III, on page 66.

COLOR

Under decisions of the United States Supreme Court, any qualification for, or disqualification from, jury service by reason of color is forbidden. The same rules apply to Grand Juries, and indictments will be dismissed if returned by Grand Juries from whose membership members of any racial group have been excluded.

CITIZENSHIP

In all states and Federal Districts, jurors must be citizens of the United States, either by birth or naturalization. Service as a juror is not permitted until final citizenship has been awarded, and the jurors must also be a citizen of the state where he is to serve. As a general rule, the lists of jurors are selected from the lists of registered voters, so the problem of citizenship seldom arises in the selection or qualification of a jury. Although the length of residence required for eligibility varies, you will seldom, if ever, be called upon to serve as a juror unless you have registered to vote at the last general election.

LITERACY

All states have a requirement that jurors be able to read and write the English language. In practice, this requirement is often overlooked, just as it is in the case of prospective voters, and it sometimes happens that a man who can barely write his name is selected to serve as a juror, particularly in states where his qualifying questionnaire is completed by a clerk or other government employee and not under the supervision of a judge.

OCCUPATIONS

Persons whose duties to the public prevent them from leaving their employment for the period of time necessary to serve as jurors usually are excused, and in some states they are actually disqualified and are not permitted to serve. Persons in such circumstances or positions will be either: (1) EXEMPT from jury duty, and excused in any case in which called to serve; (2) DISQUALIFIED, and barred from serving on any jury at any time, in any case; or (3) REQUIRED to serve. If your occupation does not appear in CHART III you may safely assume that you are required to serve. (See Page 66.)

Chapter Four

SELECTION OF THE JURY

Preliminary Selection

PRELIMINARY SELECTION

On the day of a trial, there may be as many as one hundred and fifty jurors called for examination and selection. Out of that one hundred and fifty, twelve will be selected as the jurors to try the case, with two alternates. The hundred and fifty called, however, represent only a small percentage of the number of persons eligible for jury service. The one hundred and fifty, or smaller or greater number called for a particular case are referred to as the "panel", and are selected from the jury lists of the County or Federal district in which the Court is located. Local laws, rules or regulations usually determine the number of jurors whose names are to be maintained on the jury list. The names on the jury list are usually selected from the registered and qualified voters, and the list is checked at regular intervals to replace those who have died, moved away, or for some other reason become ineligible.

Citizens who are selected for the jury list may be selected merely by having their names taken from the lists of qualified voters, and being summoned to appear on a particular day, or they may be requested to appear at the office of the clerk of the Court to answer questions, or to complete a questionnaire. In states and localities where there is a preliminary questionnaire or inquiry any juror who is disqualified, or exempt may state his reasons for being excused and thus avoid being called again. Where there is no preliminary inquiry, the notice is mailed or served by the sheriff, and on the return day the juror may state his reasons for being excused.

SPECIAL JURIES

In some states the trial of complicated or difficult cases may be held before a "Special Panel" or "Blue Ribbon" jury. In New York, for example, the Special Panels are used primarily for murder cases, and the number of names to be included on the Special Panel for each county is determined by the Judiciary Law. The names for the Special Panel are selected by lot from the names on the general jury lists, and each person selected is called to the office of the Commissioner of Jurors to complete a questionnaire. Among other questions, the applicant is asked whether he is opposed to the infliction of the death penalty, and whether he has any objections, in a proper case, to returning a verdict based on circumstantial evidence. If he is selected, his name is then placed on the smaller list of Special Jurors.

Many objections have been made to "Special Juries" as unconstitutional, and as not representing a true cross section of the community. They are sometimes referred to as "convicting juries", although public officials generally deny that there is any screening of the jurors on the basis of past performance.

SELECTION FOR TRIAL

When a number of jurors must be called for the trial of a case or series of cases, the names of all those eligible to serve (excluding those whose recent service on one or more juries has entitled them to be excused for a period of time) are placed in a large drum or wheel, and the names of those to be selected are then drawn by lot. In important cases, the lawyers for both sides are entitled to be present. After the drawing is completed, the members of the panel are notified to appear in Court.

At the opening of Court, the Court first calls for excuses, and the jurors who feel that they have valid legal excuses for absence tell the judge the reasons why they believe that they should not be required to serve in the particular case or cases. The judge will then listen to each excuse, and make his ruling immediately. An excuse of severe illness in one's family, requiring presence at home will generally be sustained, while the fact that a juror had tickets to the theater or to a baseball game will not be valid. If a juror is engaged in his own business, and the call to jury duty comes at his busiest season of the year, he may be excused from the particular panel, without prejudice to the right of the Court to call him at a later date. Each excuse will stand on its own merits, and will be determined on the circumstances of the particular juror.

After the excuses have been disposed of, the jurors will be called to the witness stand or to the jury box to be examined under oath with respect to their fitness and qualifications to serve as jurors in the case about to be tried. This preliminary examination, at the trial, is referred to as the "voir dire" examination. It usually covers all matters which tend to affect the ability of the juror to serve in the case, such as friendship or hostility to either of the parties, personal acquaintance with one of the prospective witnesses, or an aversion to the type of case being tried. In some states each juror is placed in the witness chair, and after being sworn to answer truthfully the questions asked of him, is interrogated, and at times is furnished with information which will enable him to answer the questons asked of him. In other jurisdictions, twelve jurors are placed in the jury box simultaneously, and are then questioned simultaneously. In most state courts the lawyers for the opposing sides conduct the examination, and ask the questions, while in Federal Courts the judges ask the questions, and the lawyers are free to suggest to the judge questions to be asked of particular jurors, or of the panel in general.

The purpose of the "voir dire" examination is, of course, to obtain a fair and impartial jury. The answers may show that a juror could not conscientiously serve as a juror, or that there is some reason why he would not make a good juror. If, for example, the prospective juror has been a friend of many years standing of the defendant, he could not be expected to judge impartially. On the other hand, if he himself had been injured in an automobile accident, he might be unduly sympathetic to the plaintiff in such a case. In criminal cases, the lawyers will inquire whether the jurors have ever been the victims of a crime, since a man whose house had been burglarized might be unduly prejudiced in the trial of a defendant accused of the crime of burglary.

Jurors should remember that in asking what may seem intimate and personal questions, the lawyers are merely performing a service which they are bound to do to the best of their ability. Any prying into the personal affairs of a juror is unintentional, and is done only for the purpose of protecting the lawyer's client. The lawyer will, of course, attempt to keep the questioning on the most friendly basis, since his object is to win friends and not to alienate the feelings of the juror whom he is questioning or of any other members of the jury.

CHALLENGES

A challenge is a request that a juror be excused from service in a particular case. The challenge may be for "cause", such as a prior relationship between the juror and one of the parties, a prejudice on the part of the juror or prior knowledge of the material facts of the case. A challenge for cause is addressed to the discretion of the Judge who may, if he deems the cause insufficient, overrule the challenge. In a criminal case, for example, a juror may state truthfully that he has read certain news accounts of the alleged crime. If he is challenged by the defense, the Judge may then ask him whether anything he has read would influence his judgment in the case. If the juror answers that he does not remember very much of what he read and that in any event he would put it aside and that it would not affect his judgment, the challenge for cause will probably be overruled.

There is no limit to the number of challenges for cause which may be made by either side and the lawyer is bound to exercise such a challenge whenever he feels that it is to the interest of his client or his side of the case. As a juror, you should not take any offense at being challenged, since the lawyer may like you very much personally but still feel that you should not serve on a particular case.

A peremtory challenge is one in which a juror is excused without any cause whatsoever. The challenge for bias or for cause deals with some specific known fact upon which the party urging the challenge relied to disqualify or excuse the juror. A peremptory challenge may be exercised for any reason satisfactory to the lawyer or to a party to the case, or for no reason at all. If you look at the lawyer, who is examining a prospective juror and do not like him, although you cannot tell why, the chances are that he does not like you. By the same token, if he looks at you and likes you, you probably like him. If the lawyer for some reason which you and he cannot or do not care to explain do not like each other, or if he does not like you, he can challenge you peremptorily, merely by saying "the plaintiff exercises a peremptory challenge to juror No. 6" or "the plaintiff will excuse Mr. Jones" or "defendant exercises a peremptory challenge against Mr. Williams". The form may not follow the same words in your state, but substantially the same meaning will be conveyed. The words "challenge by the defense" or "excused by the defense" mean the same thing.

Although there is no limit to the number of challenges for cause which a party may exercise or make, the number of peremptory challenges is strictly limited by law. As a juror, you need not be concerned about the number of challenges, but the lawyer will of course be required to know just how many challenges he is allowed, since without such knowledge he may very well exceed the permissible number and find himself compelled to accept jurors not to his liking.

The number of challenges varies not only from state to state, but also within your state, depending upon the nature of the case. In most civil cases, each side is allowed six peremptory challenges, while in criminal cases, the number varies from six in the comparatively minor offenses to thirty in capital cases. Where alternate jurors are selected, each side is usually allowed two additional peremptory challenges for alternate jurors in capital cases and one peremptory challenge for each two alternate jurors in civil cases. In being examined, the lawyers may through design or through inadvertence fail to ask you some questions which reveal your disqualification. Under such circumstances, you should as a matter of fairness, volunteer the information. If your business or personal situation is such that you will be greatly embarrassed by serving, you should make this fact known, both to the Judge and to the lawyers. Otherwise you may be selected for service in a case in which you should not as a matter of good conscience serve in the important capacity of passing upon the property, or liberty of another person.

Any disputes or disagreements arising between the lawyers in the selection of the jury, will be decided by the judge. You will be under oath in answering your questions and your answers to the questions may determine whether you will be challenged. As a juror, you should answer questions with the same courtesy with which they are put to you.

ALTERNATE JURORS

As we have explained in Chapter One, the usual practice in the United States is to select twelve jurors for the trial of a case. In some courts of inferior jurisdiction only six jurors are called, but these smaller juries are the exception. Where it appears that a case will take more than two days, the judge presiding at the trial may direct the lawyers to select two alternate jurors. If it appears that the case will last for more than a week, the judge usually takes this action. This practice developed in order to avoid mistrials resulting from the illness or other disability of jurors during the trial. Before the adoption of the practice of selecting and swearing alternate jurors, the judge, lawyers, and jury might sit for two or three weeks, or more, hearing evidence, and then have all their effort count for naught when one juror became ill and could not continue. In order to save the time of all concerned, and to avoid the wasted effort involved in a retrial, alternate jurors were chosen, to sit with the members of the jury and to remain with them until after the completion of the judge's charge. The alternates remain with the jury until the twelve regular members of the jury retire to the jury room for their deliberations. In the event of the illness, death or disability of a juror during the trial, and before the case has finally gone to the jury, the first alternate takes his place, while if two jurors should become disqualified for service by reason of death, disability or any other cause, the second alternate fills the otherwise vacant place on the jury.

In all but a few American jurisdictions, the verdict of the jury must be unanimous, and the jury which tries the case must consist of the full number of jurors required by law. If there is not a full jury to begin deliberations, the case may not be sent to the jury, and it will be necessary for the judge to declare a mistrial, and for the lawyers to appear at a later date, select new jurors, and present their case all over again. Before alternate jurors were selected, much time was lost through the illness or other disqualification of jurors, and the practice of selecting alternates has been beneficial both to the lawyers and their clients.

In some states the first twelve jurors selected are the ones who, barring illness, accident, death or disability, will deliberate, decide the facts, and return a verdict. In other states the jurors will all sit through the case without knowing which of them will deliberate, and after the judge completes his charge, two jurors will be selected by lot to be eliminated, with those remaining deliberating and returning the verdict. Under both systems, however, the alternates are dismissed when the jury retires, and may not replace a disabled juror once the deliberations have begun. A few years ago the mayor of a large Eastern city was indicted and tried in a spectacular proceeding lasting over fourteen weeks. After the judge's charge, and an hour after the jurors had begun their deliberations, one of their number was stricken with an attack of appendicitis and taken to the hospital, and a mistrial resulted. Had his attack come at any time before the jury had begun its deliberations, he could have been replaced by one of the alternates, and the expense and delay of a retrial could have been avoided.

DISQUALIFICATION AFTER SELECTION

If you have been selected and sworn as a juror, and in the course of your service in a particular case, something is brought to your attention which indicates to you that you should not serve, or should not have been selected in a particular case, you should report that fact to the judge. Suppose, for example, that you were told that Mary Rider, the wife of Ralph Rider, was the plaintiff, and Dave Driver the defendant. None of the names meant anything to you, and you told the lawyers and the judge that you did not know any of the parties. Much to your surprise, however, when Mary Rider took the witness stand, you recognized her as the former Mary Nevawalk, who had been your sister's best friend in high school, and at whose home you had been a guest. You should direct a note to the judge, through your bailiff or Court officer, and the judge will then report this fact to the lawyers. The lawyers may then consent to excuse you, or one of them may challenge you for cause. They may consent to your excusal and replacement by one of the alternates, or they may consent to permit the case to be tried by only eleven jurors. You should not conceal any important facts from the court, since not only may such concealment result in the inconvenience of a mistrial, but it may also subject you to criticism, censure or punishment.

EXCUSES

There may be one or more valid reasons why you cannot or should not serve as a juror. If you feel that these reasons, or any one of the reasons, are sufficient to excuse you from serving as a juror, you should present your name to the judge when you are called. Even if you are most anxious to serve, you should inform the court of the possible inconveniences, and their effect on you or on those dependent upon you. In capital cases (such as murder, rape or kidnapping) where the death penalty may be imposed, juries are sometimes locked up overnight, occasionally for the entire trial, and, more frequently on the night before deliberations begin, or after the deliberations have begun and until a verdict is returned. In some cases perplexing situations have arisen when, after a jury has been selected and sworn in such a case, one of the jurors has revealed that it would be most inconvenient to him and would work a severe hardship on other persons for him to remain away from home overnight. In one instance it was a farmer with twenty cows and no one available to milk them, in another case a man with a bedridden wife, and no one to care for her needs. You may be called for jury duty at a time when you can comfortably spare a few hours a day to perform your duty as a citizen, but you should be careful to inform the court of any factors which may affect your ability to serve faithfully throughout the entire case. As a rule, the judge will inform the jurors that it may be necessary for them to remain overnight, and if you are not asked by either lawyer, or by the judge, about the peculiar circumstances of your own situation, you should take pains to inform the Court.

In the preliminary statements made to you by the judge or by the opposing lawyers in the selection of the jury, you will be informed of the general nature of the case. You will be given enough information to let you see what kind of case it is, and if the case is one to which you have a feeling of distaste, you should ask to be excused. If the case will involve the enforcement of a law of which you do not approve, it is your duty to ask to be excused. If, for instance, you are called to serve on the jury panel from which a jury will be selected to try a defendant charged with murder, and a verdict of guilty will entail either expressly or by implication the imposition of the death penalty, you should ask to be excused if you have conscientious scruples against capital punishment. If you are called to serve on a jury in a divorce case, and you do not approve or accept laws permitting divorce, you should make this fact known to the judge and to the opposing lawyers at the time of the selection of the jury.

THE FOREMAN

In some states, the first juror to be selected automatically becomes the foreman. In other states the jurors have no foreman until after they have retired to the jury room to begin their deliberations. In either case, the foreman (or forelady, if the first juror selected, or the juror chosen by the others, is a woman) becomes the jurors' spokesman, and the presiding officer or chairman at the deliberations of the jury. It is the foreman who carries the messages of the jurors to the judge, or to the bailiff, and who often signs the notes which the jurors send to the judge requesting information or further instructions. When a verdict is reached, it is the foreman who announces the verdict, if it is returned in open court, or who signs his name first, if the verdict is a "sealed verdict" (see Chapter Six, infra) or is returned in a state or jurisdiction where verdicts are returned in written forms completed by the jurors in their jury rooms.

Chapter Five

THE DUTIES AND PRIVILEGES OF A JUROR

ATTENDANCE

The Court and the lawyers try to reduce to the barest minimum all inconveniences to the jurors. Whenever the jurors are not needed they are excused from attendance. If there is to be extensive argument on questions of law, with which the jury is not concerned, the jury may be excused for part of a session, or sometimes even for a full day or more. At times, however, jurors are required to remain at the Court even after they have completed a case, so that they will be available for selection in a new case. You should never leave the jury assembly room, or the room to which you have been summoned, without permission from the bailiff or jury officer, or from the Court. If you have some pressing personal business, or family matters which require your presence away from the Court, you should communicate the necessary information to the Court. Your prompt attendance at the opening of all sessions, and your assembly with the other jurors, as well as your remaining until you are properly and officially excused, is not only a duty of courtesy enjoined upon you by the rules of common politeness, but is also a duty imposed on you by law. For wilfull absence, lateness or tardiness, or for repeated tardiness after a warning or admonition, you may be punished for a contempt of Court, and you may be fined or imprisoned. As a general principle, the ordinary rules of courtesy and politeness are safe guides for courtroom etiquette.

SEATING

Once you have been selected as a juror in a case, you should always take the same seat in the jury box. This will not only give the lawyers and the judge a better opportunity to become acquainted with you, but will also facilitate the taking of the attendance by the clerk of the court. You should file into the jury box in the same order in which you are to sit, in order to avoid the necessity of climbing over one another or stepping on each other's feet.

In important criminal trials, such as murder, the jurors will be excluded from the courtroom until the judge has taken his seat at the bench. In other trials, the jurors are permitted to assemble right in the courtroom, in the jury box, taking their seats as they come in. In such circumstances the Court officer notifies the judge after the jurors and the lawyers have taken their seats, and the judge then makes his entrance. When the judge enters, it is your duty to rise, and to remain standing until the judge sits down, or until he tells you that you may be seated. This is a mark of respect both to the position which the judge occupies, and to the judge individually, as the incumbent of the high judicial office.

HEARING THE EVIDENCE

As a juror, it is both your duty and your privilege to hear and see every shred of evidence in any case in which you serve. If you cannot hear a witness, or cannot see some exhibit which has been accepted in evidence, you not only have the right, but you are under the duty to ask that the answer be repeated, that the witness speak louder, or that the exhibit be brought to a position where you can see it. The same applies to your hearing the judge. It is extremely important that you be able to hear everything which the judge says, and if you cannot hear him, you should immediately raise your hand, and the judge will either ask you himself why you have raised your hand, or will tell the bailiff to step over to the jury box to see what you want. You will probably notice that when an experienced lawyer is questioning a witness whose voice is low or soft, the lawyer stands at the end of the jury box, to be sure that the witness' voice carries. If the lawyer can hear the witness from a point further from the witness chair, it is reasonable for him to assume that you can hear the answers of the witness from your position in the jury box.

OBJECTIONS

The rules of evidence, governing not only what evidence may be introduced at a trial, but also the manner in which it may be introduced, have reached their present form only after centuries of evolution and change. They are the rules which experience has shown to be the most satisfactory to effect justice, and though you may not agree with them, you should nevertheless accept them implicitly as directed by the judge, and not attempt to substitute your own judgment, whim, or what you believe to be your own "common sense" or "horse sense". When a lawyer makes an objection he is doing no more than performing his duty. At times the objection may seem trivial or picayune, and, much to your surprise and annoyance, the judge may sustain the objection. If the lawyer, after hearing the other side's lawyer ask a question, rises to his feet and says "I object" or "Objection", the judge will rule upon the objection. If the judge believes that the evidence offered should not be heard, or "admitted", because its admission would be a violation of the rules by which the Court is bound, he will say "Sustained" or "Objection sustained." If the judge feels that the evidence should be admitted, and that it is proper for the consideration of the jury in deciding the case, he will say "Overruled" or "Objection overruled". On some occasions he will say "I will allow the answer." As a juror, you have no concern with the judge's ruling on objections. It sometimes happens that a witness will answer a question before the judge has an opportunity to rule. In such a case, if the judge sustains the objection, he will then instruct the jury to disregard the answer, and you should attempt to erase the answer from your mind.

At times you may feel that one of the lawyers, or both of the lawyers, are making too many objections. While this may annoy you by breaking the continuity of the story or testimony to which you are listening, it is no concern of yours as a juror. Objectons deal exclusively with questions of law, while you as a juror deal exclusively wiih questions of fact.

The rules of evidence are based on the experience of many generations of lawyers and judges. To a person not a lawyer they may seem strange and unreasonable, but you should be on your guard not to allow yourself to be prejudiced for or against one side because of objections made by a lawyer to the introduction of evidence.

DISCUSSIONS OF CASES IN WHICH YOU SERVE

If you have received a notice to appear for jury service, you should not discuss the case with anyone. In a recent murder case a juror's name was stricken from the jury list, because after receiving in the mail his notice to appear for the trial of the case, he purchased a magazine and read an article describing some of the evidence to be introduced at the trial, and then discussed the case at length with his wife and his brother-in-law. While the juror may have felt that he was getting himself better acquainted with the facts of the case, he was actually acquiring much knowledge which was irrelevant and highly prejudicial. A juror is not permitted to discuss a case on which he is sitting at any time during the progress of the case, and should limit himself to the evidence and arguments presented at the trial. At each adjournment or recess, the judge will warn the jurors not to discuss the case with each other, or with any other person, and not to permit the case to be discussed in their presence. If any outsider tries to talk with a juror about the case on which he is then sitting, the juror should not only refuse to listen, but should also report this matter to the judge at the earliest opportunity. Failure to make such a report to the judge is a serious contempt of court for which a juror may be punished severely.

Jurors should also be careful not to communicate on any subject with any lawyer or witness in a case while the case is on trial. Such a contact, while entirely innocent, is subject to misinterpretation, and may result in making a new trial necessary.

INDEPENDENT INVESTIGATIONS

As a juror, you should not try to be an amateur detective. Suppose, for example, that you are a juror in a case where the plaintiff claims that she fell down a defective stairway, and that she asks for substantial damages for her injuries. The defendant claims that the stairway was not defective. The plaintiff's witnesses all swear that the stairway was so defective that one good blast of wind would have blown it down. By the end of the plaintiff's case you are outraged that any landowner should have permitted such a death trap to exist in your community, and you feel that while you will listen patiently to the defendant's witnesses, your major concern is not so much the vast amount of money which you will award the plaintiff, but just how the defendant can be punished for permitting such a condition to exist. You wonder, in your mind, just what the judge will say, and just what instructions he will give you.

After the plaintiff "rests his case" or "rests", the defendant himself takes the witness stand, and tells how he had the stairway repaired a month before the plaintiff's injury. He then produces the contractor who swears that he repaired the stairway a month before the accident, and who adds that at the defendant's request he inspected the stairway the day after the accident, and found that it was in such sound condition that, from his glowing description, it might even withstand the blast of an atom bomb. The defendant then calls three other witnesses who swear that the stairway was sound, and then, just as you have made up your mind (although the judge warned you not to) that the defendant is a much maligned man, the defendant rests his case, and the plaintiff calls two rebuttal witnesses who testify that the stairway was examined by them the day after the accident, and was in terrible condition. One of them even adds that the contractor, whom you had appraised as a forthright witness, said in his presence, "Yes, it's in pretty bad shape." At that point court takes a recess until the next morning, and the judge tells you that on the following day the lawyers will sum up, and he will deliver his charge to the jury. You are still puzzled, and as you leave the courthouse, you get the bright idea that you will stop by the stairway, and see for yourself. You remember that you should have no contact with any of the parties, so you wait until late at night, when you are certain that no one will be around to snoop, as YOU make your inspection in the interests of justice. At midnight, you examine the stairway. You see for yourself, and by the time you are through you have even made measurements, and have made up your mind just who is not telling the truth, and just what you are going to do about it.

STOP RIGHT THERE. You should have stopped when you first had the idea, but now you have done the damage. The damage has been done to your standing as a juror. You have now received some information, or misinformation which was not available to the other jurors, and you have received it under conditions which have disqualified you from further service in the case.

What have you done wrong?

And what should you have done?

What you should have done was to write a note to the judge asking whether you, AND the other members of the jury could have a "view" or inspection of the premises. The judge would then have passed on this request, and would either have denied it, or would have directed that the Court stenographer, the jury, and the lawyers for both sides accompany him to the stairway. In all probability, he would have denied your request. What have you done wrong? You have looked at the stairway, not at the time of the accident, but at some later time, when you had no way of knowing whether it was in the same condition. It is true that you did have some testimony that the stairway was examined the day after the accident, but how do you know what happened to it in the meantime? Are you to make up your mind, from the present excellent condition of the stairway, that it was in that same condition on the day of the accident, and was not completely overhauled and repaired three months after the accident? Or are you to make up your mind that the present decrepit condition of the stairway existed at the time of the accident, and did not result from neglect or subsequent damage to the building occurring in the year and a half or (in some states, such as New York) four and five years after the accident? And what about the conditions of your observation? Was the light the same? The weather? The angle or position from which you made your examination?

You were puzzled, and as a conscientious juror, you did not realize that you were doing anything wrong. If you had waited until the next day, the judge, in his charge to you and the other members of the jury, would have told you how to reconcile the conflicting testimony, and how to decide the facts on the testimony before you.

ASKING QUESTIONS

If you, as a juror, want to ask a question of a witness, you should ask the judge's permission to do so. Such questions rarely serve any useful purpose, and usually if the juror is patient he will find the matter he has in mind included in the evidence produced by questions of the judge or lawyers. If you are afraid that a witness may have left the witness stand before you had a chance to submit your questions to the judge, raise your hand, and tell the judge that you would like to ask a question. **Do not ask the question,** since it may be so improper that it will result in a mistrial, but merely tell the judge that you would like to ask a question. The judge will then permit you to write out your question, and as the judge he will make his ruling, asking your question himself if he feels that it is proper, and telling you that he feels that it should not be asked if he believes that it is improper. If he follows the latter course, he will at some stage of the proceedings, usually after the jury has retired, or when the jury has been excused, make a statement for the record setting forth your question verbatim, and his ruling or reason for rejecting the question.

TAKING NOTES

Jurors are not permitted to take notes of the evidence they hear. While this may seem strange, the reason behind the rule is that few jurors, if any, would, or could take complete notes, and fragmentary notes would result in undue weight being given, during the deliberations of the jury, to certain facts or circumstances in disregard of others of equal importance, or in disregard of the circumstances which might affect the circumstances of the matters noted. Experience has shown that it is better to rely on the combined recollections of all of the jurors, rather than upon notes taken by one or more. If you and one or more of your fellow jurors cannot agree, in the jury room, on pertinent parts of the testimony, you may ask the judge to have read to you from the stenographer or reporter's minutes or notes, the parts of the testimony which you have trouble remembering.

RETIRING TO THE JURY ROOM

After the judge has given you charge, or instructions, you will be conducted to the jury room to begin your deliberations. You are entitled to take with you any and all of the exhibits which have been received in evidence. You are not entitled to exhibits which have merely been marked for identification. If a lawyer offers in evidence a repair bill, but does not have sufficient proof to entitle him to have the bill received in evidence, he will ask that it be marked for identification, in the hope that at some later stage of the trial he will have enough evidence to qualify the paper for admission into evidence. If the necessary evidence is not produced, the paper is never admitted into evidence, and may not be considered by the jury in its deliberations.

You will usually be instructed to take your hats and coats to the jury room when you begin your deliberations. You should follow the judge's instructions, both as to retiring as to matters which you are to consider, and the manner in which you are to consider them. If you need anything, either in connection with the case, or for your personal comfort, you may call the bailiff, and he will communicate your request to the judge.

YOUR DELIBERATIONS AS JURORS

In his instructions or "Charge" the judge will outline the law by which you are to be guided, and will also tell you the questions of fact which you are to decide. He will tell you that you, and you alone, are the judges of the facts, and that where your recollection and the judge's recollection do not coincide, yours is to control. You may find the facts in accordance with your conscience and your own common sense, and you may ignore any suggestions made by either lawyer, or any suggestion which may be implied in the judge's charge.

As we have noted in Chapter Four, in most states the first juror to be chosen serves as foreman. In a few states, no foreman is chosen until after you reach the jury room. Whether he is chosen automatically, by virtue of being the first juror to be chosen, or by the selection of his fellow jurors after they have retired to the jury room, he should preside at your deliberations, and bring your verdict into court when and if you eventually arrive at a verdict.

If at any time during your deliberations, you feel the need of further instructions or advice from the judge, you have the right, through the officer at the door of the jury room, to send word to the judge. You will then be ushered into the jury box where the foreman will state to the judge the matter as to which instructions are desired. If you cannot agree among yourselves as to the tenor of certain testimony, the judge may, upon your request, order the official stenographer or reporter to read back to you the testimony requested or part of the testimony requested. The mere request does not mean that the testimony will be read, since the judge may, in his discretion, refuse to allow the testimony to be read. If the testimony requested would take five or six hours, the judge will attempt to dissuade the jurors, or he may grant their request as to only a part of the testimony.

Your mind should, of course, be kept open until you enter the jury room. You should refrain from forming any opinion in the case until after you have received the judge's instructions. When a person has once expressed his views, he may be reluctant or hesitant to change them. It is therefore best for a juror not to commit himself until the entire story has been told. Once the entire story has been told, the juror is free to express himself **but only in the jury room.** He is under a duty to attempt to convert the other jurors to his way of thinking, and to listen to their arguments as they attempt to convert him to their conclusions. Such a situation could develop twelve reasonable men into a howling mob, and the jury will of course perform better if it has an intelligent plan to follow.

In the jury room, the twelve jurors are usually seated about a long table, like the board of directors of a bank. The foreman may say, "Gentlemen, we have heard the evidence and the charge of the court." He may then turn to the juror on his right and say "Mr. Jones, how do you think this case should be decided?", then to Mr. Smith (Juror number three), then to Mr. Williams (Juror number four) and so forth around the table. Full discussion, with an opportunity to each juror to express his opinion, should precede any vote. If you are convinced that you are wrong, you should not hesitate to change your views. On the other hand, if you believe that you are correct, you should be willing to stick by your guns, and hold to your position "until hell freezes over." If you are sitting in a criminal case, do not let yourself be plagued years later with the thought that you should not have given in, and that by your failure to adhere to a view which you felt was right, you let an innocent man be deprived of his life or liberty, or that you turned loose upon society a dangerous criminal.

You may be called as a juror in a case, either civil or criminal, where you will be called upon to apply a law of which you do not approve (as explained in Chapter Four). Your first duty in such a case is to ask to be excused from serving. If you have not realized your position, or if the judge for some reason sufficient to him has declined to excuse you, you must disregard your own feelings and decide the case on the basis of the facts presented to you and your fellow jurors. As a juror, you are not responsible for the law, and it is your duty, as it is the duty of the judge, to make your decision on the basis of the law as it is. The law will, of course, have been explained to you by the judge in his instructions or charge.

EVALUATING WITNESSES

In the case of the lady who fell on the stairway you were presented with a puzzling situation. Who was telling the truth? In order to reach a verdict, you must determine what part of the evidence you will believe, and what part you will reject as not worthy of belief. Unfortunately there is no "fool proof" way of sifting the true from the false. As yet, no one has discovered an infallible truth detector or lie detector, and in forming your opinion you must take into consideration the various factors affecting the witness which affect his credibility, or ability to be believed. You must judge the witness from your own experience in order to determine whether he is telling the truth. Did he have a good opportunity to see and hear the facts concerning which he testified, and is he sufficiently observant to have seen and heard them? How is his sight and hearing? Is he young and vigorous, or is he sufficiently along in years to have suffered some impairment in sight or hearing? Is he sufficiently intelligent to be able to remember the events which he relates? Is it reasonable or probable, considering the surrounding circumstances, that he would have seen and noted, and that he would be able to recall the facts to which he testified? Does the evidence show that the witness had a motive for favoring, or an inclination to favor, any party? In other words, was he a biased or an impartial witness? Does the story of the witness ring true? Jurors are the sole judges of the believability of witnesses, and their decision on this subject is final, and not, as a rule, subject to review by higher courts.

It is not at all unusual for witnesses to differ in some details. Such discrepancies may be due to differences in the witnesses' powers of accurate observation, or in their ability to remember what they saw, heard or did. You should try to reconcile discrepancies as far as you can, taking into account the differing capacities and capabilities of witnesses. At the same time you should consider possible causes of untrue statements, such as confusion, excitement, nervousness, mistakes, poor memory, thoughtfulness, lack of intelligence and evil intent. If a party, or a witness has a criminal record, and that criminal record is brought out during the course of the trial, you may consider it in determining how much weight to give to his testimony. Your own experience will tell you that if the conviction for an infamous crime is comparatively recent, the testimony of the witness may be viewed with suspicion, while the misdeeds of youth may long since have been lived down.

In criminal cases, the defendant may put his character in issue, by bringing before the court witnesses who know nothing about the particular charge for which the defendant is on trial, but who are in position to testify, from their knowledge of the defendant, that he has a good reputation in the community in which he lives or works. These witnesses are known as "character witnesses", and the judge will instruct you that you may consider their testimony in determining the issue of the innocence or guilt of the defendant. In reaching your conclusions as jurors, whether you have been chosen for a civil or for a criminal case, you must consider, examine and weigh all the evidence in the case, including the exhibits, if any. If you consider any part of the evidence unworthy of belief, you may disregard it. The court will also instruct you, in most states, that if you find that any witness has wilfully testified falsely as to any material fact, you may disregard all of his testimony.

CONSIDERATION OF DAMAGES AND SENTENCE

In civil cases, you must determine first whether your verdict is to be for the plaintiff or for the defendant. If your verdict is to be for the defendant, that will be the end of your deliberations, unless the defendant has pleaded a counterclaim, and has asked that he be awarded damages against the plaintiff. In the ordinary civil case, however, where the plaintiff has a claim against the defendant, and the defendant has no counterclaim, the jury must first determine whether their verdict is to be for the plaintiff or for the defendant. If the verdict is to be for the plaintiff, the jury must then determine the amount of the verdict. In arriving at the amount of their verdict, they are to be guided by the instructions of the judge, and aided by their own common sense and experience. In the case where the plaintiff sues for a broken leg and a cut on the cheek, leaving her with no disability of the leg, but with an unsightly scar across her face, the jury, if they find that the plaintiff is entitled to a verdict, will be instructed by the court to return a verdict which will compensate the plaintiff for her medical expenses, her lost wages, her pain and suffering, and for her disfigurment. If the plaintiff was a professional entertainer, or photographer's model, her losses and damages would be greater than if she were a commercial artist or a seamstress. On the other hand, if it were her leg which had been permanently injured, and she worked as a typist or switchboard operator, her damages would not be as great as if she had been a professional dancer or dancing teacher.

SENTENCES AND RECOMMENDATIONS OF MERCY

In most jurisdictions the jury has nothing to do with the sentence which is to be imposed in a criminal case. The judge usually instructs the jurors that they are to determine the innocence or guilt of the defendant, and that the sentence which the judge may or may not impose is no concern of the jury. As a juror, you should not be swayed by sympathy, or by a feeling that since the sentence will probably be light, a verdict of guilty will not make much difference. In some cases, however, you know just what the sentence to be imposed after a verdict of guilty will be. In many states conviction of murder in the first degree carries an automatic imposition of the death penalty, while in other states the death penalty is mandatory unless the jury recommend mercy — life imprisonment or imprisonment for a period of years. In New York, for example, a jury returning a verdict of guilty of murder in the first degree may recommend mercy, and the judge may (but is not required to) follow the recommendation only to the extent of imposing a sentence of life in prison. He may not impose a lesser sentence.

If you are a juror in a criminal case, you should be cautious about returning a verdict with a recommendation of mercy, and should ask specific instructions from the court if you are not entirely clear as to what the results will be. In a case tried in 1936 in a state where the death penalty was mandatory in cases of conviction of murder in the first degree, the jury asked the judge whether they were permitted to recommend mercy or leniency in the case they were deliberating, where a mother had killed her small son. The judge instructed the jurors that they were permitted to recommend mercy. The jurors returned an hour later with a verdict of guilty of murder in the first degree with a recommendation of leniency. The judge imposed the mandatory death penalty, but the conviction was reversed because the judge had failed to instruct the jury that their recommendation of leniency would have no effect if accompanied by a verdict of guilty of murder in the first degree. If you feel that there should be a recommendation of mercy, and the judge has not instructed you on that point, you should ask for instructions before you return a verdict.

GENERAL

Jurors are sometimes troubled by the thought that their decision in a particular case may have an effect which they regard as undesirable in other cases or situations. Such considerations have no place in the jurors' reaching their verdict. The members of a jury are sworn only to pass judgment on the facts in a particular case, and they are not permitted to entertain any concern beyond that particular case. If a newspaper delivery man is arrested and tried for being the runner for a gambling ring, the jurors may not take into consideration their fear that if the defendant is acquitted, they may be encouraging gambling in their locality. They are bound to consider only the innocence or guilt of the defendant on trial before them. If you as a juror render your verdict on the basis of the supposed or anticipated effect which it may have on other situations, you violate your oath as a juror.

While you are bound to lay aside all bias and prejudice, and to respect the opinions, and the right to expression of your fellow jurors, in a spirit of tolerance and understanding, you must never consent to a verdict which violates either the instructions of the court or which adopts a fact which you in good conscience believe to be untrue. You must place yourself in the position of the plaintiff and the defendant, and remember that while you sit today as a juror, tomorrow you, or someone near and dear to you, may come into court as a plaintiff or defendant, and only by the efforts of conscientious jurors can there be equal justice for all.

MEALS

In higher courts, the jurors are given their lunch on days when they sit for a full day, and their evening meal when they sit for a night session. Judges often direct night sessions if the trial is protracted. In lower courts the jurors are merely told how much time they will be allowed for their meals, and are expected to return to the Courtroom at the expiration of that interval. In the highest courts of original jurisdiction, and in most criminal trials, the jurors are taken to a restaurant for lunch by one or two officers. The officers accompany the jurors to keep other persons from talking to them, or from talking in the jurors' presence about the case, and, after ushering them to tables, sit nearby where they can watch and protect the jurors. This practice varies, and in some jurisdictions the jurors and their officers sit at the same tables, or in private dining rooms.

LODGING

Occasionally a case will be of such importance that the jury will be locked up every night until the conclusion of the trial. This happens very rarely, and is usually restricted to crimes of a most serious nature. When such a serious step is taken, the jurors are taken to the best available lodging, all provided at the government's expense. In some of the larger counties in the western states, the jurors are required to travel such long distances from their homes to the county seat, where the court sits, that they are given an allowance for lodging whenever it is necessary for them to sit overnight.

MILEAGE AND COMPENSATION

Jurors usually are paid by the day for their service. As a rule, a check is mailed to the juror at the end of his period of service for the total amount due him. The compensation varies in different states, and may be as little as fifty cents a day and as high as ten dollars a day, with payment at an even number of days. A juror is entitled to a day's pay whenever he is called to court for any part of a day, even if he is present only long enough to answer the roll call and to be sent home. Payment is made by a check mailed to the juror from the office of the state comptroller, or county treasurer. If the service lasts for more than four weeks, the juror may be given a partial payment. If the juror receives a check which he believes to be incorrect, he should communicate immediately with the office from which the check was issued.

LENGTH OF DELIBERATIONS

In some states jurors are led to the jury room at the end of the judge's charge, and left alone to "battle out" their verdict. Sometimes their deliberations last for days, and the old practice was to leave them alone, with time out for meals, until they had reached a verdict, or until they were so exhausted that they could not continue. A jury may at times find itself hopelessly divided, and unable to agree. If the vote is one-sided, either for the defendant or plaintiff in a civil case, or for the people or for the defendant in a criminal case, the court may send the jury back for further deliberations, although there is no hard and fast rule. The discharge of the jury for inability to reach a verdict is a matter within the discretion of the judge. The judge may discharge the jury, and send them home whenever he feels that they have made a sincere effort to reach a verdict, but that further efforts would be unavailing.

In Federal Courts, the practice now is for the jurors to adjourn or recess their deliberations each night, and to resume in the morning, continuing from day to day until a verdict is reached, or until it is obvious to all concerned that the powers of persuasion of all the jurors have been exhausted, and that further deliberations would not result in a verdict.

51

Chapter Six

THE JURY'S VERDICT

The word "verdict" is a corruption of the Latin words "verum dictum" or "truly said". The verdict is the truth as found by the jury. In the days when the members of the jury were witnesses rather than judges of the facts, the jurors themselves were sworn or "juré" to tell the truth, and their truth, stated or said by them, was their cerdictum or verdict. As the function of the jury expanded, and as witnesses were called by the plaintiff and defendant, and by the prosecution and defense in criminal cases, the verdict of the jury became more than a summary of what the jury themselves knew. It became not only the sum and substance of their own knowledge, but their appraisal of the testimony of the witnesses who appeared before them.

As the original jurors were almost exclusively neighbors, they did not take kindly to the absolute rejection of the statements or testimony of one of their number. Disagreements and discrepancies were resolved by slight modifications, partial rejections and partial acceptances. The verdicts were phrased in such a way as to cause no resentment, and to be acceptable to all members of the jury. From these neighborly considerations there evolved the principle of unanimity of verdict.

UNANIMITY OF VERDICT

We have seen that not all of the countries in which the jury system is used require that the verdict of the jury be unanimous. With the exception of Louisiana, however, the states and Federal Courts all require unanimous verdicts in felony cases. A felony is a serious crime, subject to different definitions and descriptions in the different states, but almost always classified as a crime punishable by confinement in a state prison for a year or more. In Louisiana, in cases where a sentence of confinement at hard labor is mandatory, nine jurors out of the twelve who sit must concur in order to constitute a verdict. In capital cases, where the death penalty is involved, there are no exceptions, in American jurisprudence, to the rule requiring the verdict to be unanimous.

In less serious criminal cases, there are a few exceptions to the rule, and in Oklahoma a conviction of a misdemeanor may be had on the concurrence of three-fourths of the jury. In Montana and Idaho a jury may return a conviction, in misdemeanor cases upon the concurrence of two-thirds of its members.

Ordinarily a trial by jury requires the submission of the case to a full jury. If a juror becomes disabled, and there has been no alternate chosen at the start of the trial to replace him, the result is a "mistrial", and the entire case must be tried all over again. Texas juries are permitted to continue, without the necessity of a mistrial, or retrial, if one or two jurors become disabled. In connection with unanimity of verdict, removal or replacement of a member of a Court Martial (which is in effect a military jury) see Chapter Seven.

In civil cases the rules requiring the concurrence of all jurors for a verdict have at times proved unworkable and cumbersome. When the jury, after a sufficient time devoted to deliberations, has been unable to agree on a verdict, they may report to the judge that they are unable to agree upon a verdict. If the judge believes that they have made every conscientious effort possible under the circumstances, and the difficulty of the case, to arrive at a verdict, he may, in his discretion, discharge the jury and declare a mistrial. The mistrial, as we have seen, requires the entire case to be retried, before a new jury. With the increase in the number of jury trials in the past forty years, it became increasingly clear that it would become more and more difficult to convince twelve men or women that they should agree, and there was an alarmingly large number of jury disagreements, or "hung juries". Much time and money was wasted by the retrial of cases where ten or eleven jurors had been unable to convince one or two diehards who stuck to their guns. This was particularly true in cases involving automobile accidents or collisions, and involved cases where there was a ten to two or eleven to one division for both the plaintiff and for the defendant.

The defendant in a criminal case is not greatly inconvenienced by a disagreement or hung jury. The worst that it means for him is a retrial. The experienced criminal lawyer usually attempts to select, for the jury which will try his client, men with as many, and as widely different backgrounds and experience as possible. With a jury composed of men of different ages, occupations, religions and ancestries, the district attorney's chances of attaining a meeting of twelve minds are considerably less. The district attorney in a criminal case, and the plaintiff's lawyer in a civil case, in those states which still require unanimous verdicts, must convince twelve jurors of the righteousness of their side of the case. The defendant's lawyer, to prevent a verdict from being returned against his client, needs only one juror. The defendant's lawyer, if he cannot obtain a verdict in favor of his client, hopes for a mistrial. A series of mistrials means that his client does not go to jail in a criminal case, and does not have to pay any money in a civil case. As long as the verdict is not returned against the defendant, he wins. The plaintiff, on the other hand, cannot win unless a verdict is returned in his favor.

Even the defendant in a civil case, while he is not required to pay any money in the event of a hung jury, and the resulting mistrial, is still under the expense and obligation of defending a case where the majority of the jury wanted to find in his favor. In order to minimize, as much as possible, the expenses of retrials, there has been a departure in civil cases, in some states, from the rule of unanimous verdicts, and jurors are now permitted to return a verdict, in certain states, as soon as five-sixths of them have agreed.

The fact that a juror does not concur in the finding for the plaintiff in a civil case does not mean that he is precluded from participating in the discussions and deliberations relative to the amount of the verdict, but before the verdict may be returned to the courtroom, the required number of jurors must agree. In a state permitting a verdict to be returned on the concurrence of five-sixths of the jurors, five-sixths must agree not only as to the party in whose favor the jury is to return a verdict, but also as to the amount.

RETURNING THE VERDICT

When the jurors are taken to the jury room for the purpose of deliberating on the evidence, they are under the custody of a bailiff or court officer. The officer guards the jury room, and permits no one to enter or leave. The jurors, whenever they desire to communicate with the judge, knock on the door which the bailiff or officer has locked, or signal him by pressing a button. In most states the jury's verdict is reported orally to the judge, but in a few states the jurors complete and sign a written form in the jury room, and then return with it to the courtroom. Where a written report is required, the jury foreman tells the officer that a verdict has been reached, but does not tell him what the verdict is. The officer then furnishes the form, which the jurors complete and sign, with the foreman signing his name first. The form states the party in whose favor the verdict has been agreed upon, as well as the amount on which the jurors have agreed.

In states where the jury still reports its verdict orally, the foreman calls the officer, and tells him that the jury has agreed upon a verdict. The foreman does not tell the officer what the verdict is, but reserves that information for the judge. After being informed that a verdict has been arrived at, the officer notifies the judge, who calls the lawyers to their places at the counsel table, in the courtroom. The jury is then brought into the Courtroom, and the judge asks them: "Gentlemen of the jury, have you arrived at a verdict?" The foreman then speaks for the jury, and answers, "Yes, your Honor, we have." The judge then asks, "How do you find?" And the foreman then answers, in a civil case, "We find for the defendant" or "We find for the plaintiff in the amount of ....", stating the amount upon which the jury has agreed.

In criminal cases, the colloquy is very much the same, with the foreman stating, "We find the defendant not guilty" or ". . . guilty of . . ." or "guilty with a recommendation of mercy."

In either case, the attorney for the losing party will then ask that the jury be polled, and the clerk of the court then asks the jurors to listen as their names are called, and to state whether the verdict returned by them jointly is the verdict of each individually. After the jury has been "polled", the jury's function has been completed. The lawyers will still be busy making motions, the winning party to enter a judgment on the verdict of the jury, and the losing party to move to set aside the verdict. These are technical matters with which the jury has no concern. Unless he considers their verdict to have been outrageous, and against the weight of the evidence, or induced by some misconduct, the judge will thank the jury for their service, and give them further instructions. If they have completed their tour of service, he will then dismiss them, and tell them that they may go to their homes. If they have not completed their tour of service, he will tell them when to return to the Courtroom, or to proceed to another room in the courthouse for selection in another case.

SEALED VERDICTS

Occasionally the jury will receive a case at a comparatively late hour, and the lawyers and the judge will leave the courtroom, instructing the jury to return a "sealed verdict". The jury will be conducted to its room, under the supervision of an officer, who will guard the entrance to the jury room. When the jurors have arrived at a verdict, they write a note to the judge, telling him what their verdict is, and then, after all members of the jury have signed the note, it is sealed and handed to the officer. The jurors are then permitted to leave the Courthouse, and at the opening of court the next day, or the next Court day if a weekend or holiday has intervened, the jurors assemble in the courtroom, and their sealed verdict is opened by the judge, and read by him into the record. After this has been done, the procedure is the same as in cases where the verdict has been returned orally.

FINALITY OF THE VERDICT

The losing side will almost invariably move to set aside the verdict, and this motion presents a question of law with which the jury has no concern. The judge has a certain amount of power over the verdict of a jury, but he may not substitute for that of the jury his own estimate of the truthfulness or lack of truthfulness of any witness or group of witnesses. He may, in certain circumstances, set aside the verdict where the facts, as found by the jury, do not justify a judgment in accordance with the jury's verdict as a matter of law, and in other circumstances he may set aside the jury's verdict where it is so much at variance with the facts presented to the jury that it is clearly "against the weight of the evidence", or where it is incredible. While this situation does arise from time to time, the judge usually accepts the verdict of the jury, even though he may disagree with the findings.

IMPEACHING THE VERDICT

IMPEACHING THE VERDICT—A juror may not testify to anything that took place in the jury room for the purpose of showing that the verdict was arrived at through mistake or misconduct. The basis for this rule which bars a juror from impeaching his own verdict is the finality of the administration of justice. If a juror could testify to some irregularity or error, jurors would be harassed by the defeated party in an effort to secure from them something which might invalidate the verdict and result in a new trial. This would make the jurors' deliberations, which are intended to be private, a public record, and the subject of constant investigation. It would not only lead to interminable litigation, and uncertainty as to the termination of litigation and the results of trials, but would also tend to destroy all frankness and freedom of discussion in the jury room. A juror might not speak with frankness if he felt that his judgment, however strongly he believed it to be correct, might be the subject of a long and public review, where he might be subjected to a public examination or cross examination.

The jury's verdict must be arrived at, not as the result of chance, or lot, but after mature and considered deliberation. In a case reviewed by the United States Supreme Court, one of the jurors had offered to testify that the verdict had been arrived at, not as the result of a consideration and deliberation upon the evidence presented at the trial, but by each juror writing down on a slip of paper the amount which he thought the plaintiffs were entitled to recover, and by then dividing the total by twelve, and announcing the result as their verdict. The Court held that the testimony could not be admitted, and said that in reaching such a result, it was forced to choose between righting the wrong which had been done to private litigants and inflicting upon the public, injury which would result if jurors were permitted to testify to what went on in the jury room in the course of reaching a verdict.

In the event of the wilful misconduct of a juror, however, the jurors may testify in criminal prosecutions against the offending juror or jurors, but their testimony will not ordinarily be permitted to impeach the verdict. If, for example, a juror in a criminal case were to announce at the beginning of the deliberations that he had made up his mind before the case started that the defendant was guilty, or innocent, and had then refused to listen to the other jurors, or to state any reasons for his position, he could be prosecuted for contempt of court, but the verdict of the jury as a whole would not be affected by the misconduct of a minority. In such a case, the testimony of the other jurors would be admissible, or competent to show the misconduct of the offenders, but inadmissible, and incompetent to impeach or set aside the verdict.

Chapter Seven

MILITARY JURIES

COMPARISON OF MILITARY AND CIVIL COURTS

—In the administration of justice in the Armed Forces, there is no such thing as a Civil Court or tribunal which can award money damages in favor of one party and against another. The only courts which exist for the trial of cases are courts-martial which determine the innocence or guilt of members of the Armed Forces on charges brought against them. Sometimes courts-martial and military commissions have jurisdiction over persons who are not members of the Armed Forces, but who are serving with the Armed Forces in the field, attached to them, or who happen to be within the jurisdiction of the Armed Forces by reason of the occupation of territory by the United States.

Courts-martial are appointed by military commanders. Summary courts-martial, which try minor offenses, consist of one officer; special courts-martial which try more serious offenses consist of any number of members (enlisted or commissioned, or both) not less than three, while general courts-martial which try serious crimes consist of a law officer and any number of members (enlisted or commissioned, or both) not less than three, while general courts-martial which try serious crimes consist of a law officer and any number of members (enlisted or commissioned, or both) not less than five.

In civilian courts we may have, and in fact have had, cases of a bank president or public official being tried by a jury composed of laborers and farmers. In trial by courts-martial, however, no member of the Armed Forces may be tried by any person junior to him in rank, if such a circumstance can be avoided. An officer may be tried only by a court-martial composed entirely of officers, although in some circumstances, an officer may be superior in rank to one or more of the officers on the court before which he is tried. A warrant officer may be tried only by a court-martial composed of officers, or of officers and warrant officers, and an enlisted person, if he desires enlisted members on a special or general court-martial, may make a request before trial that the membership be composed of not less than one-third enlisted persons.

During World War II, enlisted persons did not serve on courts-martial, and the change of the law in the 1948 Articles of War, permitting enlisted persons to serve as members of a court-martial, was hailed as a great step forward. The provision, however, has rarely been availed of by enlisted persons who prefer officers on the courts-martial before whom they are to be tried. Various theories have been advanced for this practice, but the most plausible seems to be that among enlisted persons assigned to court, the majority would be first sergeants or master sergeants in the Army, Marine Corps and Air Force and Chief Petty Officers, or First Class Petty Officers in the Navy and Coast Guard, and would be much less sympathetic than junior officers to enlisted persons who were absent without leave or who were charged with desertion or misbehavior before the enemy.

LIMITATIONS ON POWERS OF MILITARY COURTS

—The Summary Court Martial, which consists of only one officer as the judge of both the law and the facts, may not properly be called a military jury, whereas the Special Courts Martial and General Courts Martial are in effect military juries. A Summary Court Martial, which tries only minor offenses, may impose confinement not in excess of one month, hard labor without confinement not in excess of forty-five days, restrictions to limits for a period not in excess of two-thirds of one month's pay. Special Courts Martial, which consist of three or more members, deliberate and serve as the judges of the facts, and to a certain extent, the law. The President of a Special Court Martial, who occupies his position as president by virtue of being the senior officer or members present, retires with the Court to take part in its deliberations, but prior to retirement, or closing of the Court for deliberation, he serves as the "Judge" and rules on questions of law and objections. He fills the position occupied at a General Court Martial by the Law Officer, with the exception that the Law Officer does not retire with the Court, and does not take part in its deliberations.

A special Court Martial tries offenses which, while more serious than the petty violations or offenses which are tried by a Summary Court Martial, are still considered minor offenses. The Special Court Martial may adjudge any punishment except death, dishonorable discharge, dismissal, confinement in excess of six months, hard labor without confinement in excess of six months, forfeiture of pay exceeding two-third pay per month, or forfeiture of pay for a period in excess of six months. A Special Court Martial may impose a bad conduct discharge.

A General Court Martial may try any offense recognized as a violation of the Uniform Code of Military Justice, and may impose any punishment it sees fit, as long as such punishment is authorized by the Uniform Code of Military Justice. Only a General Court Martial, among Military Courts, may impose the death penalty, a dishonorable discharge, or dismissal from the service.

SELECTION OF MEMBERS OF COURTS MARTIAL

—Members of Courts Martial are selected or designated for service by military orders issued by the appropriate military commanders. A military commander is authorized to appoint as members of Courts Martial those members of his command who are in his opinion, best qualified for the duty by reason of age, education, training, experience, length of service, and judicial temperament. It is even possible for a Court Martial to be composed of members of more than one of the Armed Forces, although the better practice is to have the Court consist of members of the same Armed Forces as the person to be tried.

Since a Special Court Martial must have at least three members and a General Court Martial at least five members, sworn to participate in the trial of a case, the convening authority (the military commander who appoints the Court by issuing a military order) usually appoints several more than the required minimum, in order to allow for some members to be excused, absent or removed by challenges.

In the manner of selection, military juries, or Courts-Martial differ somewhat from civilian juries, which are selected by lot from the lists of qualified persons. Military juries are selected not by lot, but by specific selection from

61

the members of the command whom the commander or his representatives feel will be the best suited for the important task. The commander will be scrupulously careful in the selection of the court, since any inefficient proceedings or outrageous verdicts will reflect unfavorably on his command. He may go over the list of members selected to serve, and eliminate those who have been members of courts which have returned unduly severe verdicts, or verdicts which were not warranted by the evidence. He may also provide for instruction sessions, at which the members of the court are advised by the staff judge advocate of the extent of their duties. This instruction and familiarization of laymen with legal procedures tends toward a more expeditious disposition of the cases eventually tried by the Court.

CHALLENGES—A law officer may be challenged only for cause, while a member of the Court, whether Special or General, may be challenged either for cause, or peremptorily (see page 29). In civilian courts, the judge rules on all challenges, and the members of the jury have nothing to say about the challenge addressed to their colleague. In military courts, however, it is the members of the Court (in effect, the military jury) which passes upon the sufficiency of challenges for cause. A challenge for cause may be made by either the prosecution or the defense, and the party making the challenge may call witnesses in support of his challenge, and may examine the member challenged. The other side may then cross examine, and call its own witnesses in order to defeat the challenge. After both sides have adduced their evidence in support of, and in opposition to the challenge, deliberation and voting upon the challenge will take place in closed session, and the members will vote by secret written ballot. The vote will be in the form of "Sustained" or "Not sustained", and a majority of the members voting will decide. If there is a tie vote, the challenge is sustained, and the member challenged is disqualified. The challenged member will not vote or take part in the deliberations. If the minimum number of members (five for a general court-martial, and three for a special court-martial) is present, the remaining members (four in a general court martial and two in a special court martial) may vote upon the challenge.

VOTING AND DELIBERATIONS—Deliberations by the members of courts martial in closed sessions includes a free and frank discussion and members are forbidden to use the superiority of rank in any manner in an attempt to control the independence of members in the exercise of their judgment.

Voting is by secret written ballot, and all members are obliged to vote. The members mark their ballots "Guilty", "Not guilty", or "Not guilty, but guilty of............................" inserting a lesser included offense of which they may feel that the accused is guilty, although not guilty of the more serious offense with which he is charged.

For a conviction to be returned by a special court martial, two-thirds of the members present must concur in a finding of guilty. If nine members sit on the court, and only five vote for conviction, the accused is acquitted. In computing the number of votes required for a conviction, a fraction is counted as one; thus, if five members are entitled to vote, a requirement that two-thirds concur is not met unless four members concur.

The same rules apply to general courts martial, however, with the exception that in any case in which the death penalty is mandatory, no person shall be convicted unless all members present, at the time the vote is taken, concur. After the verdict on the issue of innocence or guilt has been determined and announced, the court will be opened to hear evidence on the question of punishment. Unlike civilian juries, which only occasionally, and in only a few jurisdictions, determine the sentence, the military jury, or court martial always determines what sentence is to be imposed on the accused after he has been found guilty.

The court martial before being closed to deliberate and vote on the sentence, hears evidence which will assist it in fixing the punishment. It considers collateral matters such as the value of the property stolen in the event of a larceny case, the length of absence without leave where that is the offense charged and the previous convictions of the accused, his prior behavior and the chances of his rehabilitation. These are matters which in civil courts are left entirely to the Judge. The court may also accept hearsay evidence and unsworn instruments or letters in behalf of the accused but is careful to safeguard the rights of the accused by excluding unsworn evidence against him.

The Court sits at closed session during deliberation and voting upon the sentence with only the members of the Court present. Deliberation will include the same full and free discussion as in the determination of guilt or innocence. After there has been a complete discussion any member of the Court who desires to propose a sentence writes his proposal on a slip of paper. The junior member then collects the proposed sentence and submits them to the president. The court then votes on the proposed sentences beginning with the lightest sentence proposed until a sentence is adopted by the concurrence of the required number of members. Voting on each proposed sentence is by secret written ballot and in each case the junior member collects and counts the votes. The count is then checked by the president who announces the results of the ballot to the members of the Court. Each member of the Court is bound to vote for a proper sentence for the offense or offenses of which the accused has been found guilty without regard to his opinion or vote as to the guilt or innocence. Any sentence, even in a case where the punishment is mandatory, must have the concurrence of the required number of members.

No person may be sentenced to death by a court-martial except by the concurrence of all of the members of the court present at the time that the vote is taken and no person may be sentenced to life imprisonment or to confinement for a period in excess of ten years, unless three-fourths of the members present concur. All other sentences are determined by the concurrence or agreement of two-thirds of the members present at the time the vote is taken. The same rules of computation, that is, counting a fraction as one, apply to the votes on sentence as to the votes on the issue of innocence or guilt.

For the information of the command authorities who appointed the court, but not as a part of the sentence itself, the court may include in the record a brief statement of the reason for its sentence.

As soon as the sentence has been determined, the court will open, and the president will announce the sentence in the presence of the law officer, the accused, and counsel for both sides. He does not report the exact number voting for conviction or acquittal but merely states that the required number concurred. The court may not reconsider the sentence with a view to increasing its severity, but may correct its sentence upon proper instructions by the law officer if the sentence is not in accordance with the law.

The members of the Court may, if they desire, submit a recommendation for clemency. A specific example occurred in the case of a soldier in Korea convicted of involuntary manslaughter by the accidental discharge of his weapon. The court sentenced him to dishonorable discharge and confinement at hard labor for one year but urged clemency to the convening authority, who suspended the execution of the sentence and after a suitable period of time remitted the penalty and restored the soldier to duty, upon the recommendation of the court which imposed the sentence.

APPENDIX

APPENDIX

CHART III

OCCUPATIONS EXEMPT, DISQUALIFIED AND

REQUIRED TO SERVE AS JURORS

ALABAMA:
Excluded: Persons convicted of infamous crimes. **Exempt:** Teachers, attorneys, druggists, doctors, clergymen, firemen, policemen.

ALASKA: Compiled Laws, Article 2, §§55-7-21 to 55-7-88.
Exempt: Judicial officers, civil officers, attorneys, clergymen, physicians, teachers, members of the armed forces or of the militia.

ARIZONA: Arizona Code of 1939, §§37-102 et seq.
Excluded: Persons convicted of a felony, persons unable to read, write and understand the English language. **Exempt:** Persons over 60, civil officers, clergymen, physicians, dentists, teachers, attorneys, newspaper editors, school employees, railroad employees.

ARKANSAS: Arkansas statutes, §§39-205 to 39-208.
Exempt: Persons over 65, physicians, dentists, clergymen, ferry keepers, road overseers, school directors, constables, undertakers, firemen.

CALIFORNIA: Title 3, Chapter 1, Article I to XII, §§190-264, California Code of Civil Procedure.
Excluded: Persons not residing in the State for one year. **Exempt:** Judicial officers, armed forces officers, public officers, teachers, attorneys, physicians, dentists, chiropodists, members of the militia, railroad employees, clergymen, seamen.

COLORADO: General Statutes, Chapter 95, §§1 to 57.
Exempt: Firemen, railroad employees, postal employees, persons observing Saturday as Sabbath.

CONNECTICUT: General statutes of Connecticut, Chapter 388, §§7906-7928, Supplement to Page 388, §§1359b to 1368b.
Excluded: Persons under 25. **Exempt:** Firemen, Fire Department Engineers, members of state assembly, attorneys, physicians, members of the militia.

DELAWARE: Revised Code, Chapter 131, §§1 to 33.
Excluded: Attorneys, public officers, clergymen, dentists, physicians, teachers, pharmacists, veterinarians, undertakers, bank cashiers.

DISTRICT OF COLUMBIA: Dist. of Columbia Code Title 11-1401 to 11-1423.

Excluded: Persons over 65, persons unable to read, write and understand English, persons convicted of felony or misdemeanors involving moral turpitude. Exempt: Judicial officers, members of the Armed Forces, policemen and firemen, attorneys, clergymen, physicians, employees of hospitals and asylums of charitable institutions, captains, masters and employees of ships navigating in District of Columbia waters.

FLORIDA: General Statutes, Chapter 40.01 to 40.43.

Excluded: Public officers, sheriffs and deputy sheriffs, assessors, tax collectors, county treasurer, clerks of the court. Exempt: attorneys, newspaper men, teachers, physicians, dentists, pharmacists, clergymen, one miller to each mill, one ferry man for each ferry, firemen, employees of state institutions.

GEORGIA: Georgia Code, Title 59-101 to 9901.

Exempt: Clergymen, physicians, pharmacists, dentists, teachers, millers, ferrymen, railroad employees, telegraph operators, persons over 60, pilots of vessels, policemen, stationary engineers, railroad postal clerks, embalmers, members of the armed forces.

HAWAII: Revised statutes, §§9791 to 9813.

Excluded: Persons unable to read and write English, persons convicted of felony, or misdemeanors involving moral turpitude or persons who have violated a public trust. Exempt: Persons over 60, attorneys, public officers, clergymen, teachers, physicians, dentists, seamen, members of the militia.

IDAHO: Idaho Code Title II, §101, Title II, §603.

Excluded: Persons not registered as voters, or convicted of felony or offenses involving moral turpitude. Exempt: Public officers, attorneys, teachers, employees of public utilities, physicians, express agents, druggists, railroad employees, persons who have served within one year, firemen.

ILLINOIS: Jones statutes annotated, §§107.225, 107.227.

Excluded: Persons not understanding English, persons of bad character. Exempt: Public officers, clergymen, attorneys, physicians, pharmacists and their assistants, ferrymen, policemen, firemen, undertakers and embalmers, newspaper employees and volunteer firemen with seven or more years of service.

INDIANA: Burns Indiana statutes, 4, 3301 to 3325.

Excluded: Persons inelligible to vote. Exempt: Persons over 60, persons serving within one year, ferrymen, firemen, members of militia, policemen.

IOWA: Code annotated, Chapter 607, 607.1-607.6.

Excluded: Persons ineligible to vote, persons not familiar with English language. Exempt: Attorneys, physicians, dentists, pharmacists, embalmers, nurses, chiropodists, osteopaths, veterinarians, teachers, firemen, persons over 65, persons having religious bias against jury service.

KANSAS: General statutes, Chapter 43, §43-101.

Excluded: Persons not qualified to vote, persons who have served within one year, persons convicted of felony. **Exempt:** Members of the militia, persons over 65, clergymen, physicians, dentists, pharmacists, attorneys, teachers.

KENTUCKY: Revised statutes, 29.010-29.990.

Exempt: Persons over 60 years of age, public officers, physicians, dentists, pharmacists, school teachers, attorneys, telegraph operators, firemen, volunteer firemen, clergymen, railroad employees, policemen.

LOUISIANA: General statutes, Chapter 37.

Excluded: Persons who have not resided in State for one year. **Exempt:** Public officers, attorneys, clergymen, physicians, teachers, druggists, firemen, telegraph operators, engineers of sugar refining factories.

MAINE: Revised statutes, Chapter 103.

Excluded: Persons who have served within three years. **Exempt:** Public officers, attorneys, teachers, clergymen, physicians, nurses, Fire Department engineers.

MARYLAND: Ant Co Article 51.

Exempt: Persons over 70, public officers, physicians, pharmacists, teachers.

MASSACHUSETTS: Consolidated Laws, Page 234.

Exempt: Public officers, attorneys, clergymen, teachers, physicians, persons under 25 years of age, members of volunteer militia, employees of public institutions, railroad conductors and drivers, firemen.

MICHIGAN: Statutes annotated Chapter 266, §27.

Exempt: Public officers, teachers, clergymen, railroad superintendents, engineers, conductors, ferrymen, firemen, members of the Michigan National Guard, pharmacists, physicians, dentists, persons over 65.

MINNESOTA: Statutes annotated 593-628.

Exempt: Persons over 60, public officers, clergymen, teachers, physicians, ferrymen, telegraph operators, one miller for each mill, embalmers, firemen, engineers.

MISSISSIPPI: Code annotated Chapter 9.

Excluded: Persons convicted of a felony or misdemeanor. **Exempt:** public officers, attorneys osteopaths, dentists, teachers, engineers, keepers of public mills and ferries, chiropractors, attorneys, telegraph operators, one druggist per drug store.

MISSOURI: Revised statutes, Chapter 5.

Exempt: Volunteer firemen, paid firemen, employees of state institutions, clergymen, physicians, dentists, attorneys, ferrymen, druggists, road overseers, embalmers.

MONTANA: Revised Codes of Montana, Chapter 13, §§93-1301 to 93-1307.

Excluded: Persons unable to speak English, persons not owning property and persons convicted of a felony, persons under 21 and over 70 years of age. **Exempt:** Public officials, attorneys, clergymen, teachers, physicians, druggists, dentists, embalmers, undertakers, employees of public institutions, express agents, National Guardsmen, railroad superintendents, nurses actually on duty.

NEBRASKA: Revised statutes of Nebraska, Chapter 25, §§1601-1638.

Excluded: Clerks of Court, persons convicted of an offense permitting imprisonment. **Exempt:** Public officers, attorneys, physicians, dentists, pharmacists, postmasters, members of the Militia or Armed Forces, employees of public institutions.

NEVADA: Compiled laws, §§8476 to 8482.

Exempt: Public officers, attorneys, teachers, dentists, physicians, pharmacists, engineers actually engaged in positions where their presence is required, letter carriers, all paid firemen, one-half of the voluteer firemen in each fire company.

NEW HAMPSHIRE: Revised Laws, Chapter 375, §§1 to 29.

Exempt: Public officers, judges and clerks of court, registers of deeds, sheriffs and deputies, attorneys, clergymen, physicians and dentists, postmasters, engineers, firewardens and firemen, persons over 70.

NEW JERSEY: Statutes 2A: 85-1 to 2A: 96-7.

Excluded: Persons over 65, persons with less than two years residence, persons convicted of crime, public officials concerned with the administration of justice, persons unable to read or write English, disabled or infirmed. **Exempt:** Fish and game wardens, physicians, dentists, custodians of minor children, employees of state institutions, members of the militia, telegraph employees, teachers, firemen and volunteer firemen with seven years service.

NEW MEXICO: General Statutes 30-101 to 30-137.

Excluded: Residents of less than a year, persons convicted of bribery or infamous crimes. **Exempt:** Federal, State, District and County employees, physicians, dentists, druggists, funeral directors, embalmers, members of the National Guard, attorneys, clergymen, teachers, persons over 60 years of age.

NEW YORK: Judiciary Law, Article 16, 17, 17A, 18, 18A, 18B.

Excluded: Persons over 70 years of age, persons not owning property of a value of $150.00, elective officials, public officers; judges, court clerks and deputies, sheriff and deputies. **Exempt:** Clergymen, doctors, dentists, licensed pharmacists, licensed embalmers, optometrists, members of the Armed Forces, National Guard or Militia, firemen, policemen, pilots, newspaper editors and employees.

NORTH CAROLINA: General Statutes, Division II 9-1 to 9-31.

Excluded: Persons of bad moral character, persons convicted of crimes involving turpitude, persons adjudged incompetent. **Exempt:** Physicians, druggists, telegraph operators, pilots, clergymen, employees of state hospitals, funeral directors, embalmers, printers and linotype operators, millers of grist mills, postal employees, locomotive engineers, trainmen, conductors, radio broadcasters and announcers, practical nurses, attorneys, national guardsmen, members of Armed Forces and reserve components, women required to care for minor children.

NORTH DAKOTA: Statutes §§27-0901 to 27-0903.

Excluded: Judges, sheriffs, coroners, jailers, attorneys, infirm persons, persons convicted of offenses punishable by imprisonment. **Exempt:** Persons over 60, clergymen, public officers, teachers in public schools, court clerks, physicians, dentists, pharmacists, postmasters, letter carriers, members of organized fire companies.

OHIO: General Code, Division III, §§11419-1 to 11431-1.

Excluded: Exclusions and exemptions are granted in the discretion of the Commissioner of Jurors.

OKLAHOMA: Statutes Title 38; constitution §§18 and 19.

Excluded: Persons not qualified as voters, persons of unsound mind, judicial officers, sheriffs, constables, jailors, attorneys, drunkards, persons disabled, persons convicted of infamous crimes. **Exempt:** Persons over 60, clergymen, County and District officials, physicians, dentists, undertakers, pharmacists, public school teachers, postmasters and letter carriers, members of the National Guard, newspaper employees, firemen, women with minor children.

OREGON: Compiled Laws, Title 14-101 to 312. Constitution Art. VII.

Excluded: Persons of unsound mind, persons convicted of crime involving moral turpitude. **Exempt:** Judicial officers, public employees, attorneys, physicians, dentists, chiropodists, osteopaths, Christian Science Practitioners, naturopaths, undertakers, optometrists, firemen, members of legislature.

PENNSYLVANIA: Purdon's Pennsylvania Statutes, Title 17, §§911 to 1330.

Excluded: Persons unable to understand English, persons under indictment or convicted of crime, attorneys and physicians. **Exempt:** Guardians of the poor, members of the Pennsylvania Reserve Militia, operators and employees of telegraph companies, members of the National Guard, veterans of the National Guard and United States military service.

RHODE ISLAND: (1923) General Laws, Chapter 506, 1 to 39.

Excluded: Persons under 25. **Exempt:** Members and officers of the assembly, wardens and superintendent of State institutions, judicial officers, sheriffs and deputies, public officers, policemen, firemen, volunteer fire chiefs, clergymen, attorneys, doctors, druggists, osteopaths, chiropractors, optometrists, pharmacists, faculty and students of Rhode Island State College, Brown and Providence Colleges, town clerks, pilots, undertakers, persons over 70, federal employees.

SOUTH CAROLINA: Code of Laws of South Carolina, Title 38, 1 to 410.

Excluded: Court employees and attaches, Judicial officers, persons convicted of infamous crimes. **Exempt:** Federal, State, County and Municipal employees, clergymen, physicians, druggists, embalmers, attorneys, persons over 65, railroad employees, dentists and dental hygienists, women.

SOUTH DAKOTA: Code §§32.1001 to 32.1014.

Excluded: Persons unable to read, write and understand English, Judges, public officers, attorneys, jailers, infirm and disabled persons, serving within two years, persons over 70, persons convicted of a felony. **Exempt:** Persons excused by the Court.

TENNESSEE: Code of Tennessee, Chapter 5, 9984 to 10049.

Excluded: Persons related within the sixth degree to litigants, persons convicted of infamous crimes, persons not in full faculties of hearing and sight. **Exempt:** Federal and State employees, railway mail service employees, attorneys, physicians, clergymen, teachers, firemen and members of fire companies, persons over 65, pharmacists, members of National Guard.

TEXAS: Texas Revised Civil Statutes, Article 2133, 2134, 2135.

Excluded: Persons not qualified to vote, persons not freeholders, persons unable to read and write English, persons who have served within six months, persons convicted of a felony. **Exempt:** Persons over 60, public officers, clergymen, physicians, attorneys, newspaper publishers, school teachers, druggists, undertakers, telegraph operators, railroad station agents, ferrymen, millers at saw, grist and flour mills, presidents, vice presidents, engineers, firemen and conductors of railroad companies, firemen.

UTAH: Judicial Code, Part V 78-46.1 to 78-46.33.

Excluded: Persons unable to read or write English, persons not paying taxes, persons of unsound mind or bodily disability, persons convicted of malfeasance in office or any felony, officers or soldiers of United States Armed Forces. **Exempt:** Federal, State, Judicial and Civil officers, members of National Guard, County, City, Town or Precinct employees, attorneys, editors, teachers, physicians, employees of public institutions and hospitals, express agents, mail carriers, telephone and telegraph employees, ferrymen, gate keepers, druggists, supervisory engineers, railroad employees.

VERMONT: Statutes, §§1720-1734.

Excluded: Persons convicted of felony, resident of municipality when municipality is party to an action, poor persons. **Exempt:** Doctors, clergymen, attorneys, members of National Court, State officers.

VIRGIN ISLANDS: Title 5, Chapter 12, General Ordinances.

Excluded: Persons convicted of a felony, persons under 25 years, persons not qualified to vote. **Exempt:** Judicial officers, physicians, dentists, clergymen, attorneys, civil officers.

VIRGINIA: Code of 1950, §§8-174 to 8-208.

Excluded: Idiots, lunatics, persons convicted of bribery, perjury, embezzlement of public funds, treason and felonies or petty larceny, inmates of charitable institutions. **Exempt:** Public officers, physicians, optometrists, osteopaths, dentists, judicial officers, telephone and telegraph employees, train dispatchers, pilots, elected officers, post office employees, mariners, teachers and students, clergymen, sheriffs, harvesters (during harvest season), public hospital and institution employees, policemen, ferrymen, undertakers, members of the National Guard.

WASHINGTON: Revised Code of Washington, 2.36.010 to 2.36.160.

Excluded: Non-voters, non-taxpayers, persons not familiar with the English language. **Exempt:** Federal and State employees, attorneys, school teachers, physicians, embalmers, firemen, policemen, persons over 60.

WEST VIRGINIA: Code §§5261 to 5298.

Excluded: Persons over 65, persons of unsound mind, habitual drunkards, persons convicted of infamous crimes. **Exempt:** Attorneys, physicians, dentists, pharmacists, post office employees, Judicial officers, Federal, State and County officers, members of the National Guard, Telegraph operators, clergymen, employees of public institutions, railroad engineers, members of organized fire and police department, teachers, pupils.

WISCONSIN: Statutes Chapter 255, §§270.15 to 270.32.

Excluded: Persons not qualified as voters, persons unable to read and write English, persons convicted of felony. **Exempt:** Elective state officers, judges and clerks of courts, City and County officers, constables, employees of State institutions, member of National Guard and veterans of 5 years service discharged for disability, attorneys, physicians, dentists, clergymen, presidents and cashiers of banks, teachers and school and college instructors, one miller to each grist or saw mill, factory foremen and engineers, one druggist in each drug store, telegraph operators, railroad, express and canal company employees, one ferryman for each ferry.

WYOMING: General Statutes, Chapter 12, 12-101 to 12-145.

Excluded: Persons over 65, persons with less than one year's residence, persons not possessing ordinary intelligence, persons not familiar with the English language, persons convicted of malfeasance in office or felony. **Exempt:** Judicial officers, military officers, County, Town and Township employees, attorneys, clergymen, editors, teachers, physicians, druggists, employees of public or charitable institutions, express agents, letter carriers, telegraph employees, national guardsmen, fire department members, railroad engineers and conductors.

JURORS' GLOSSARY

Action—A legal dispute brought into court for trial.

Answer—The paper in which the defendant answers the claims made by the plaintiff.

Argument or Summation—The arguments or speeches of the lawyers on each side to the jury after all the evidence has been submitted. In this argument, each lawyer tells the jury what he thinks the evidence proved and why he thinks his side should win. This is referred to as an "argument", "summing up", "summation", "closing statement", or "closing".

Case—The same as action. A legal dispute brought into court for trial or determination.

Cause of action—The legal grounds upon which a party to a law suit bases his claim or case.

Challenge, Challenge for Cause or Bias—a request by a lawyer for one side, to the Judge to excuse a juror on the ground that there is ample cause or reason for the belief that the juror cannot render an impartial verdict or should not with propriety sit on the case.

Charge or Instructions to the Jury—The outline by the Judge of the rules of law which must guide the deliberations of the jurors and control their verdict. This is sometimes referred to as the "Judge's instructions", or the "Judge's summing up to the Jury."

Civil Case—A law suit or action between persons in their private capacities or relations.

Complaint—The paper in which the plaintiff or plaintiffs (the persons who bring the law suit or action) set forth their claims against the defendant.

Counterclaim—A claim by the defendant in his answer to the complaint that he is entitled to damages or other relief from the plaintiff.

Criminal Case—A law suit or case where the people of a state or the people of the United States of America, are the plaintiff and a person or corporation is named as a defendant. A criminal case involves a question of whether the defendant has violated one of the laws defining crimes. The verdict is not stated as "for the plaintiff" or "for the defendant" but as "guilty" or "not guilty".

Cross Examination—The asking of questions of a witness or parties to an action by the lawyer for the opposing side. The "cross-examination" follows the "direct examination."

Defendant—The person against whom a law suit is started and against whom a claim for relief or damages is made. In a criminal case the person charged with an offense is called the defendant.

76

Defense or Affirmative Defense—The matter upon which the defendant relies to resist or defend the claim of the plaintiff. The defense may be a "general denial" under which the defendant denies the claims of the plaintiff or it may be an "affirmative defense" under which he admits some or all of the facts or while denying some or all of the facts, nevertheless claims that there are other affirmative matters which should relieve him from responsibility.

Deposition—The testimony of a witness reduced to writing in question and answer form. This testimony is usually taken by court order out of court, because a witness due to illness or other cause, cannot be produced at the trial.

Direct Examination—The asking of questions of a witness or party to the action by the lawyer for the party. The examination of a witness by the lawyer who calls him is his "direct examination."

Directed Verdict—An order by the Judge to the clerk to enter a verdict as a verdict of the jury. This will be done when the evidence presented by both sides has been heard and shows that there is no issue of fact for the jury to decide, but only an issue of law to be decided by the Judge.

Examination in Chief—Direct examination.

Exhibits—Articles such as pictures, books, letters, knives which are used in evidence. These are called "exhibits" and are generally given to the jury to take to the jury room while deliberating.

Issue—A disputed question of fact. It is sometimes referred to as "one of the questions" which must be answered by the jury in order to reach a verdict.

Mistrial—A declaration that proceedings are a nullity and that a new trial must be begun de novo. It may be caused by a disagreement by the jury or by some circumstance beyond the control of the party.

Motion—A request by one of the lawyers for a ruling on a point of law. A motion is decided by the Judge and not by the jury.

Objection—A protest or objection by a lawyer to the introduction of evidence or to certain conduct in the course of an action.

Objection overruled—The rejection by the Judge of an objection made by a lawyer. In overruling an objection, the Judge states that in his opinion the lawyer was not correct in objecting to the introduction of evidence.

Objection Sustained—The agreement by the Judge with the lawyer who made the objection. This results in the evidence offered being excluded.

Opening or Opening Statement—A short speech or statement by the lawyer to the jury at the start of the case, telling the jury what the case is about and what evidence he expects to bring in to prove his case.

Parties—The people who are involved in the case. The plaintiff and the defendant. They are sometimes called the "litigants".

Peremptory Challenge—A request by a party (either plaintiff or defendant) that a juror's name be stricken from the panel which is to try the case. No reason is required to be stated for a peremptory challenge and it may be exercised for any reason whatsoever.

Plaintiff—The person who starts a law suit or case.

Pleadings—The paper in which the parties state their claims and defenses. The pleadings are the complaint, the answer and the reply.

Record of Minutes—The word for word transcript or report of the proceedings of a trial made by the official reporter.

Reply—The plaintiff's answer to a counterclaim or affirmatives defense pleaded by the defendant in his answer.

Rest—Sometimes stated as "plaintiff rests" or "defendant rests" or "both sides rest". This is a legal term which means that the lawyer has completed the evidence which he wants to introduce at the particular stage of the trial. When "both sides rest", the case is closed, except for the arguments of the lawyers and the instructions of the Judge, both preceded by motions by the lawyers.

Trial—The process of determining a dispute in Court. The parties present their evidence and the Judge and jury try or hear the case and render a determination.

Verdict—The finding of the jury. A sealed verdict is the sealing of the verdict in an envelope and the bringing of the envelope into the Court at a later session.

INDEX

A

Adultery, 11
Age, 22
Air Force, 59
Alabama, 66
Alaska, 66
Alternate Jurors, 31
Arizona, 66
Arkansas, 66
Armed Forces, 59
Army courts, 60
Assessors of damages, 18
Assistant District Attorney, 18

B

Ballot, 8
Ballot wooden, 2
Blue ribbon jury, 26

C

California, 66
Capital cases, 33
Challenges for cause, 29
Challenges—generally, 29
Challenges—military, 62
Charlemagne, 8
Citizenship, 25
Civil Status, 24
Clemency, 48
Coast Guard, 59
Color, 24
Colorado, 66
Columbia, District of, 67
Compensation, 50
Complaint, 14
Connecticut, 66
Constitutional right, 10, 11
Coroner's Jury, 19
Counsel, 11
County Clerk, 24
Court Clerk, 24
Court Martial, 59
Courts, Military, 59
Convicting Juries, 27
Cross Examination, 16

D

Damages, 18, 47
Death—sentence by Military
    Court, 64

D (cont.)

Defendant, 12
Delaware, 66
Deliberations, 44, 51
Direct Examination, 15, 16
Discussions, 39
Disqualification, 34
District of Columbia, 67
Doomsman, 8
Duties, 39

E

Enlisted persons, 60
Examination, cross, 15, 16
Examination, direct, 15, 16
Evaluating witnesses, 46
Evidence, bearing, 38
Excuses, 27, 33

F

Federal Court, 28
Finality of verdict, 57
Fitness, 28
Florida, 67
Foreman, 34

G

General Court Martial, 60
Georgia, 67
Grand Jury, 5, 19

H

Hawaii, 67
Hearing evidence, 38

I

Idaho, 67
Illinois, 67
Impeaching the verdict, 57
Indictment, 19
Information, 19
Iowa, 67
Investigations, 39

J

Juré, 9
Jury, definition, 5

K

Kansas, 68
Kentucky, 68

L

Length of deliberations, 51
Limitation on Military
  Courts, 60
Lodging, 50
Louisiana, 68
Literacy, 25

M

Maine, 68
Marine Corps, 59
Maryland, 68
Massachusetts, 68
Meals, 50
Mercy, recommendation, 48
Michigan, 68
Mileage, 50
Military Courts, 59
Minnesota, 68
Misdemeanor, 19
Mississippi, 68
Missouri, 68
Montana, 69
Murder, 27

N

Navy, 59
Nebraska, 69
Nevada, 69
New Hampshire, 69
New Jersey, 69
New York, 69
No bill, 6
Normans, 9
North Carolina, 70
North Dakota, 70
Notes, 42

O

Objections, 38
Occupations, 25
Ohio, 70
Oklahoma, 70
Opening statements, 15
Oregon, 70

P

Pennsylvania, 70
Peremptory Challenges, 29
Plaintiff, 12
Pleadings, 13, 14
Preliminary examination, 28
Preliminary selection, 26
Privileges, 36
Prosecutor, 5

Q

Qualifications, questions, 28
Questions, 27, 28
Questions by Jurors, 42

R

Rebuttal, 18
Recommendation of Mercy, 48
Resting a case, 16
Returning the verdict, 56
Retiring to deliberate, 43
Rhode Island, 70

S

Scabini, 8
Sealed verdicts, 56
Seating, 36
Selection for trial, 28
Sentences, 48
Sentences, military, 64
Sex of Jurors, 20
  Chart, 21, 22
South Carolina, 71
South Dakota, 71
Special Court Martial, 60
Special Juries, 26
Summary Court Martial, 60

T

Taking notes 42
Tennessee, 71
Texas, 71
Tribal Jury, 6
True bill, 6

U

Unanimous verdict, 52
Utah, 71

V

Vermont, 71
Verdict, 52
Virginia, 72
Voir dire, 28
Voting, 44
Voting, military courts, 63

W

Washington, 72
West Virginia, 72
Wisconsin, 72
Witnesses, 46
Women as jurors, 20
Wyoming, 72